WITHDRAWN

William Hare believes that open-mindedness – the disposition to form a belief, and if necessary to revise or reject it, in the light of available evidence and argument – stands in need of a defence because it is under widespread attack. In this sequel to his highly regarded *Open-mindedness and Education* (1979), he examines the numerous ways in which opposition to open-mindedness is expressed, and shows how these criticisms can be countered. He argues that the general indictment of open-mindedness as a habit of mind leading to nihilism and scepticism, as well as to neglect of the emotions, is based upon a misunderstanding of the nature of the concept, which in his opinion is by no means incompatible with personal commitment and confidence. Similar confusions are exposed in such areas as elementary schooling, moral education, educational standards, methods of teaching, the administration of schools, and the teaching of science. In each of these areas, examples are taken from the writings of influential critics to illustrate the nature of the doubts concerning open-mindedness – doubts that are carefully analysed and shown to rest ultimately upon erroneous assumptions. And since he believes that many who set out to champion open-mindedness manage to confuse this ideal with other notions, Hare undertakes in a concluding chapter to protect the ideal from its would-be friends and supporters.

William Hare is Professor of Education and Philosophy at Dalhousie University. Among his recent publications is *Controversies in Teaching*.

In Defence of
Open-mindedness

WILLIAM HARE

McGill-Queen's University Press
Kingston and Montreal

© McGill-Queen's University Press 1985
ISBN 0-7735-0580-6 (cloth)
ISBN 0-7735-0581-4 (paper)

Legal deposit 2nd quarter 1985
Bibliothèque nationale du Québec

Printed in Canada

Canadian Cataloguing in Publication Data

Hare, William
    In defence of open-mindedness
    Includes bibliographical references and index.
    ISBN 0-7735-0580-6 (bound). – ISBN 0-7735-0581-4 (pbk.)
    1. Teachers – Attitudes. 2. Education – Philosophy –
    1965– I. Title.
    LB1025.2.H36 1985   371.1′001′9   C85-098403-3

This book has been published with the help of a grant from the Social Science Federation of Canada, using funds provided by the Social Sciences and Humanities Research Council of Canada. Publication has also been assisted by the Canada Council and the Ontario Arts Council under their block grant programs.

To my father

Contents

Foreword

In this volume, William Hare continues his long-term scholarly engagement with the idea of open-mindedness for the benefit of all of us. Open-mindedness is a fundamental and fecund idea in western liberal thought, both educational and political. In Hare's treatment, it is at once a saint-like attitude of fairness and willingness to consider other views and a dogged commitment to reason, evidence, and truth.

Hare's arguments are sharp and his willingness seriously to consider a host of arguments from a vast literature which stretches across disciplinary boundaries but is always relevant to education attests to his own exemplary commitment to open-mindedness. Without a sophisticated concept of open-mindedness like Hare's, we who have inherited the Enlightenment beliefs in individual autonomy and the sovereignty of reason and evidence would stand on the brink of relativism – or worse, nihilism – hoisted on our own petard. Hare's thoughtful and thorough work provides a way out.

There is much talk nowadays about teaching people how to think critically. I think teaching people the attitude of open-mindedness will do more to foster critical thinking than any of the more direct, how-to approaches. Hare serves the educational community (and our culture at large) well with his important work. The book is a monument to his ideal and deserves a careful and open-minded reading.

Jonas F. Soltis
William Heard Kilpatrick Professor of
Philosophy and Education
Columbia University

Preface

In *Open-mindedness and Education,* I set out the main features of the attitude of open-mindedness and showed how this attitude is related to the idea of education and to various methods of teaching and subject areas. Some attention was paid to various doubts about the possibility of such an attitude; and the final chapter looked at a series of objections which might be raised against it in the teaching context. But the opposition to open-mindedness, to the claim that it is both possible and desirable, is much more extensive than I managed to suggest, or indeed fully appreciated at the time.

It turns out, for example, that many philosophers and educational theorists who genuinely place a high value on open-mindedness think that the attitude is objectionable in specific contexts. These include certain levels of education, such as the elementary or primary school context, certain areas of inquiry, such as reflection on our basic moral principles in practical situations, and certain roles in education, such as that of administrator. Moreover, it is felt that important educational practices, such as curriculum planning, assessment, and the framing of objectives, undermine the possibility of open-mindedness in education. The difficulties encountered here have spawned a host of simple-minded solutions which masquerade as open-minded approaches, such as equal time theories and dogged neutrality.

There are also those who simply do not value open-mindedness, thinking that its links with rationality entail an approach to education which ignores the emotions, and which leads inevitably to a situation in which nothing is valued. The arguments presented are superficially plausible and appear to have attracted a sizeable following, and it is clearly important to attempt to rebut this position. It is dangerously misguided to pretend that no one seriously advances such views. Some will see this as a defence of that which needs no defence, but others will see it as a defence of the indefensible. It is this split which makes the study important.

In short, the aim of the present book is to advance the study of open-mindedness and related concepts by showing what the attitude requires in a variety of contexts, and by demonstrating that it does not succumb to the many objections raised. The thesis is that open-mindedness is presumptively good, and that the presumption cannot be overturned as readily and as often as is suggested. The ideal of open-mindedness does not have to be abandoned because certain practices in education are followed.

A work of this sort, which seeks to defend an ideal under attack, is bound to be incomplete. One can never identify, and deal with, all the objections which have been raised, let alone anticipate those which might be raised. I hope, however, that it can be fairly claimed that the most serious and frequently canvassed objections have been examined.

Any book which ventures into several areas of philosophy as this one does also runs the risk of being judged superficial. In dealing with certain issues in ethics and philosophy of science, for example, I am well aware that there is an enormous literature which has remained untouched. I would be satisfied, however, if I have succeeded in saying enough to call into question the popular belief that open-mindedness can be safely relegated to the museum which houses extinct ideas.

I have chiefly aimed at making a contribution to the philosophy of education, and hope to have shown how the notion of open-mindedness is fundamental to the concept of education. It is both possible and desirable as an aim of education, and I have tried to bring out the way in which conceptual confusion hinders the appreciation of this truth.

Versions of chapters 1, 2, 4, and 8 have appeared as articles in the *Oxford Review of Education, Elementary School Journal, European Journal of Teacher Education*, and *Educational Philosophy and Theory*. I am grateful to the editors of these journals for allowing me to utilize this material here. A version of chapter 3 was presented to the Department of Education seminar at Dalhousie University in October 1981, and chapter 5 was presented at the annual meeting of the Atlantic Philosophical Association, Université Ste Anne, November 1983. I have received valuable comments from the two referees appointed by the Social Science Federation of Canada, and from the reader appointed by McGill-Queen's University Press. I am once again indebted to both the Federation and the Press for their assistance and cooperation at each stage of the publication process. I began the work for this book during a six-month sabbatical leave from January to June 1981. During this time I was partially supported by a Leave Fellowship from the

Social Sciences and Humanities Research Council of Canada. I wish to thank Dalhousie University for granting me leave during that period. I have been fortunate to receive excellent secretarial assistance from Thérèse Boutilier. As ever, my wife Niki has been a constant source of advice and encouragement.

In Defence of Open-mindedness

... all rational creatures go out upon the sea of life with their minds made up on the common questions of right and wrong, as well as on many of the far more difficult questions of wise and foolish.
John Stuart Mill, *Utilitarianism*

Thus I arrived ... at the conclusion that the scientific attitude was the critical attitude, which did not look for verifications but for crucial tests; tests which could refute the theory tested, though they could never establish it.
Karl Popper, *Unended Quest*

CHAPTER ONE

The Attack on Open-mindedness

THE BACKGROUND

It is now fashionable to regard as naive in the extreme any attempt to promote open-mindedness as an educational ideal. We have heard much in recent years about the hidden curriculum, the inevitability of bias, the political nature of educational decisions, and the impossibility of cross-cultural judgments, to refer to just a few popular and influential sceptical arguments in this context. The defender of open-mindedness is faced with a veritable network of arguments, anyone of which is thought to be decisive against such a position. And collectively, the effect is to make this enterprise appear hopelessly misguided. Indeed, the espousal of open-mindedness is itself seen as an instance of being locked into a particular, culturally relative framework.

This sharp division, into those who identify open-mindedness as an educational ideal and those who see it as a futile illusion, is nevertheless based on, and in part made possible by, general agreement about the meaning of the concept. Despite the fact that there is considerable disagreement about the presuppositions and implications of the concept, it is widely held that open-mindedness involves a willingness to form and revise one's views as impartially and as objectively as possible in the light of available evidence and argument. The fashionable view is just that there are insuperable difficulties built into this. It is important, however, if we are to get the arguments here into perspective, to realize that those who defend open-mindedness have no wish to claim that it is easy to attain. This is indeed recognized in referring to it as an ideal, though it would be going too far to read into this the view that it can only be approached but never achieved.

In particular, it must be admitted that it is all too possible that we will fall short of impartiality and objectivity. To say that this is possible, however, is not to say that it is inevitable, though the frequency of this move, and the confidence with which it is made, would indicate that this elementary distinction is not widely recognized. What is true is that a serious attempt to be open-minded may lead us to form views which are false, to give up views which happen to be true, or to continue to hold others which ought to be abandoned. In short, the attitude cannot guarantee that we will conduct our thinking well. And yet, for anyone with a concern for truth, anxious to arrive at true, reasonable, or morally sound conclusions, there must be a *presumption* in favour of open-mindedness. To ignore objections and criticisms which might show that a certain view is false, or bring into sharper focus the truth it contains, is to show a disregard for truth.

Such a presumption, of course, does not mean that open-mindedness is *always* desirable. For example, the likelihood of making the right decision in certain cases may be so remote if we try to evaluate all the circumstances, that we may decide to stick with a well-established general principle. Again, in wartime, the open-minded consideration of the claims of the enemy may give indirect support to the enemy, and thus may be judged to be less important than other attitudes.[1] The onus may well fall on the person who wishes to defend closed-mindedness on a given occasion to make out his case, but it is entirely possible that this could be done. If the presumption is not defeated, however, a concern for truth will require serious consideration of evidence and argument in the formation or revision of one's views. The extent to which a vigorous search for evidence and argument is demanded will reflect the general context, including the importance attached to being right in the particular case, and the likelihood of others confronting one with objections and criticisms. Clearly, there will be great variation here. But whereas the advocate of free expression is not under a special obligation to acquaint himself with the content of the views which he is not prepared to have silenced,[2] the open-minded person must be willing to consider them and be prepared to be influenced by them in his thinking. The attitude of open-mindedness commits one to comparing rival views.

COMPARISON AS DISTORTION

It is at this point that we encounter a radical objection to open-mindedness. The concession above that open-mindedness does not necessarily lead to the truth, and the admission that the claims of open-mindedness can be outweighed on occasion by other considerations, will be dismissed as beside the point. It will be held that in some sorts of cases, the open-minded consideration of views must necessarily frustrate the pursuit of truth, and introduce an element of distortion. This kind of argument is quite different from that argument, now part of the conventional wisdom, which holds that we are always liable to distort matters through bias and prejudice even if we are sincere. The argument to be considered here is that comparative assessment itself involves distortion, with the result that an impartial and objective assessment is impossible. Open-minded consideration is itself prejudicial.

Suppose, for example, we bring to mind "the potentially awkward fact that it is possible to hold, as a matter of moral conviction, that certain topics should not even be discussed."[3] The problem which this fact generates is not that in discussing an issue we may in fact be less than fair to a particular point of view, but that in discussing it at all one rides rough-shod over the views of some. It must be said at once, and clearly, that the open-minded individual is not required to be determined to discuss an issue whatever disagreements there may be. Teaching strategies need to take into account probable consequences, and it is not difficult to imagine circumstances in which discussion would very likely be counter-productive. And the open-minded teacher is not bound to be insensitive to the feelings of those who oppose the discussion. On the other hand, we must also insist that if the discussion goes ahead, it does not follow that the views of the opposition are inevitably distorted. The discussion can call attention to the fact that some sincerely believe that the discussion should not occur, and possible reasons for this view can be explored. If they are not explored, we could not know whether or not we should agree with them, and some consideration is necessary, therefore, to determine this. We might conclude that we were wrong to discuss the issue, and in this way the opposition could be vindicated.

Consider a related case, in which a certain group holds that there is no obligation to give an open-minded hearing to the views of one's opponents. Would not any open-minded consideration of this point of view necessarily undermine it? In response to this, it must be admitted that in giving consideration to this point of view we are in practice rejecting it. But this does not prevent us from attending to whatever arguments might be advanced in favour of that view. Our practice does not show that we do not take the view seriously, only that we do not accept it. Open-mindedness demands that we be fair to a view, but we are not bound to support a view in order to be fair to it.

The comparative analysis of concepts is also thought to make for distortion. Here the view is foisted on the philosopher that "clear concepts describe reality more accurately."[4] Now, it is certainly the case that many philosophers would allow that the clarification of concepts is an important part of their task. It consists in charting those logical connections which hold between and among concepts, and which make for their complexity. But this does not mean that an *exact* distinction can always be drawn. There is not, for example, an exact point at which open-mindedness turns into closed-mindedness, and this is because these concepts have an element of vagueness built into them. For most important philosophical concepts, it is not possible to provide a precise analysis in terms of a complete set of necessary and sufficient conditions. In setting out to compare two concepts, however, we are not bound to assume that the distinction between them can be precisely stated, nor that individually they can be fully analysed. We might even find that what we took to be different concepts were not different at all. If it is true that "philosophers have allowed their keenness for precise distinctions to override their concern for accuracy,"[5] this is no more than an occupational hazard. We have no cause to harbour suspicions about the process itself. Our clarification may consist in bringing out the fuzziness and vagueness in the concepts. Incidentally, the observation that, for example, all indoctrination includes some teaching,[6] does not cast doubt upon the appropriateness of conceptual comparison here. To say that there is an important conceptual distinction between indoctrination and teaching is not to maintain that there is no overlap between these concepts, but only to insist that they are by no means equivalent. If, in fact, the boundaries are drawn too sharply, then we must look to a more accurate analysis to bring this out. Sometimes, of course, it will be useful to suggest a tighter notion than analysis reveals, though it will be important to make clear that we are prescribing.

Our open-mindedness is not compromised by drawing, or suggesting, certain distinctions, or in maintaining that some other view is false. We are not committed to holding that other opinions are just as good as our own. Such a mistake seems to explain Niemeyer's objection to comparing the political systems of the United States and the USSR in American schools: "... it should be rejected because it avoids the central problem posed by communism, that of evil at the heart of a political regime ... Comparison between the Soviet system and ours thus begs the very question it is supposed to answer."[7] The question which it is thought such a strategy will inevitably beg is whether or not the two systems are comparable, in the sense that they are different, but equally acceptable political systems. To take this view would be, according to Niemeyer, to fail to attend to the all-important difference between the two, that is, that the Soviet system is, at bottom, evil. But there is no reason at all why comparative assessment must beg this question. We can admit that the two systems are political systems and can be compared as such. To say this, however, is not at all to say that they are much the same, or different but equally acceptable. Comparative assessment, after all, permits the drawing of *contrasts*, and may well in this case support Niemeyer's judgment. Moreover, how could one assess this judgment if a comparison were not made? Does not Niemeyer's own view quoted above itself involve a comparison? We may come to the conclusion, and nothing in the strategy rules this out in advance, that "there is no comparison" between the two systems, meaning that one is infinitely preferable to the other; but it is a simple confusion to think that this in any way justifies the view that a comparative assessment is not appropriate.

Furthermore, as many philosophers have pointed out,[8] we cannot seriously assert a value judgment and maintain at the same time that any other conviction will do equally well. Thus, where incompatible value positions are taken in different political systems, the "different but equal" attitude is excluded. This logical necessity, however, should not lead us to conclude that we can only have a closed mind about value judgments which conflict with our own. This substantive view does not follow from the purely logical point. We can be willing to consider objections to our value judgments, and be prepared to revise our views in the light of these. It is, I think, potentially misleading to say that when we make value judgments, "we must for the time being put on one side our anthropological spectacles through which we survey the conflicting opinions of the human race."[9] Certainly, we must abandon the relativism which is fallaciously thought to follow from anthropology, but we can continue to bear in mind the fact that quite different views are sincerely maintained by others. This does not leave us divided in our minds, for we can be confident that we are right, yet prepared to change our views should it emerge that we are wrong.

The correct observation that a value judgment commits the person who makes it to rejecting value judgments which conflict with it, is appealed to in order to establish the conclusion that it is not possible to be humble about one's own values.[10] If correct, this would be damaging in two ways. First, a widely proclaimed virtue of a critical approach is exposed as a myth. And second, since humility is thought to be a necessary feature of open-mindedness, this too is either impossible or something very different from what it is typically portrayed to be. And since the point about value judgments can be applied to other sorts of claims, the doubt about open-mindedness applies in a quite general way. The open-minded stance then distorts the fact that we are committed to certain values.

But what is the force of this objection? Certainly, if we claim to know something, or subscribe to a value position, ours cannot be the humility of the despairing voice which asks, for example, which version of modern history or of philosophy we are to teach. Let us further agree that an assumption of infallibility would make humility an unlikely virtue at least. But there are many intermediate positions here. When we claim to know something is true or right, we can regard our view as *vulnerable*, and can, therefore, possess that humility which recognizes other points of view as potential sources of defeat for our own position. This amounts to a kind of respect for other views, though it does not entail relativism. We must now turn to examine those arguments which suggest that critical questioning ultimately leads to the destruction of values.

CRITICISM AS NIHILISTIC

Sometimes, it is true, arguments against such critical values as impartiality, detachment, open-mindedness, and so on, appear in the context of an attempt to show that one can over-emphasize these values to the neglect of others. We have already seen that open-mindedness is not the only, nor the supreme, value, and thus the danger of an over-emphasis can readily be granted. Nevertheless, in the course of arguing for this correct view, many fallacious arguments are given which purport to show that the family of concepts considered here is fundamentally suspect. It is alleged that they lead to a situation in which nothing is valued.

One very tempting line of thought here suggests a connection between open-mindedness and doubt. A plausible connection of a psychological kind has, of course, been suggested by many writers and there is a good deal of truth in the observation that a person who is utterly convinced that he is right is unlikely to pay attention to the criticisms and objections of others.[11] But can a connection of a logical kind be shown to hold? Phillips and Mounce, for example, suggest that "if we are one of the parties involved in a moral disagreement, it is queer for us to ask, having taken our stand, 'And who is right?' If we do ask this question it is an indication of doubt on our part."[12] The point here is that, if indeed we are sure about our principles, no further questions remain to be asked. It is conceded that a person might be impressed by an opponent's degree of conviction, and be inclined to review the whole matter. But this sounds like a case in which some doubts have set in. What needs to be stressed here is that one could conduct such a review without abandoning, or weakening, one's conviction during or after the review. And this would not call into question the seriousness of the process. Many factors can prompt such a review, including our general awareness of our own fallibility, the complexity of the issue, and so on. To pay attention to doubts expressed by others, or to those which we try to imagine, is not to doubt one's own view. There is a sense of "questioning," such as in the statement "I question that," which conveys doubt or even rejection, but not all questioning implies this.

The importance of addressing the doubt thesis is simply that it is seen as the first step on the road which leads to what Feinberg has called "that corruption of the ideal of open-mindedness where everything is always 'up for grabs'."[13] Therefore, it is important to look at the most uncompromising statement of the doubt thesis in recent philosophy, which is captured in the following claim: "One thing which must be entirely absent and which is, I think, implicit in the absence of all doubt, is this: any openness on the part of the man to consider new experience or information as seriously relevant to the truth or falsity of the thing."[14] Open-mindedness on this view presupposes doubt. But is it in fact the case that, if I have complete confidence in my views, open-mindedness is excluded? Or, as others have claimed,[15] that my entering a *discussion* about these views would be quite unintelligible? Surely, a person earns the right to be completely confident as his view continues to withstand criticism. My emerging confidence does not mean that I am unwilling to abandon my view, only that I do not expect to have to do so. I may indeed enter into a discussion for the purpose of actively looking for difficulties in my view, even if I feel sure that none will emerge.

Unger argues that being absolutely certain of something implies closed-mindedness or, as he puts it, dogmatism, an absolutely severe attitude in which "*no* new information, evidence or experience will now be seriously considered by one to be *at all* relevant to any possible change in how certain one should be in the matter."[16] Unger allows that a person who has no doubts now about something can consistently admit that he may change his mind should certain evidence come up, but points out that this involves a shift away from a consideration of the person's present attitude to a prediction of what he will, or might, do in certain circumstances. I do not wish to dispute the claim that the attitude described by Unger entails the absence of open-mindedness. But is this attitude involved in being absolutely certain? Suppose that a person cannot see, or imagine, how his present view could be defeated.[17] His inability to see how there could be relevant counter-evidence (which justifies his absolute certainty) does not mean that his present attitude is that *he will count nothing* as contrary evidence. He is prepared now to abandon his view if counter-evidence should emerge, though what this might be like he cannot say. It will be helpful here if we reject the view expressed by Peirce that "when doubt ceases, mental action on the subject comes to an end; and, if it did go on, it would be without a purpose."[18] It can very well have that purpose which Socrates was concerned to point out to Meno, namely ongoing reflection on our beliefs.[19]

The notion of detachment is an obvious source of confusion. It is thought to be dangerous, for it is supposed to leave others who have no scruples about indoctrination a free hand to impose their values. Moreover, it is thought to be spurious, and to entail nihilism.[20] The following assertion provides a clue to the confused thinking which lies behind these claims: "To be committed to impartiality, to criticism and to 'truth for its own sake' is to be committed to not being committed."[21] Thus the critical values are seen as implying a detachment in which nothing is valued in the end. Surely, the mistake here arises from confusing not being committed in advance, or defiance, of relevant evidence, with not being committed to anything whatever. To be committed to the values in question here is to be determined to have one's beliefs rationally grounded, not to have no beliefs at all. There is no *reductio* here. Any superficial cleverness rests on a failure to state the *kinds* of commitments an open-minded person will avoid.

Again, we are warned that "a thoroughgoing commitment to critical questioning can, however, lead one in this direction, towards valuing less and less as one achieves greater and greater degrees of detachment."[22] It is, no doubt, true that one could ignore many values and ideals in pursuing certain goals. But this is a case of neglect. It is not one's thoroughgoing commitment to critical questioning which necessitates this. Indeed, if one is seriously committed to critical questioning, one must think that the answers matter, for these give point to the questions. And the questions may concern our beliefs, our values, our emotions, *and* our priorities. If we have our priorities wrong, then we might properly say that our commitment to critical questioning has not been sufficiently thoroughgoing. We have failed to raise certain kinds of questions.

It might perhaps be objected here that some philosophers have explicitly said that in some contexts, in philosophy for example, the questions are more important than the answers. But this would, I think, be to interpret an epigram as a thesis. Certainly, there is an important point being made here, for a good question opens up avenues of exploration previously neglected. And in philosophy, definitive answers are hard to come by. Having allowed all this, however, it remains true that good questions here, as elsewhere, are those which lead to further understanding. Indeed, a good question can encapsulate a new way of looking at things, and in philosophy this is one important aspect of progress.

Another aspect of detachment arises in connection with the distinction mentioned earlier between analysis and prescription. That there is such a distinction is clear enough, for we may agree about the meaning of some concept yet have very different recommendations to make about it. Since these matters *are* different, philosophers have properly insisted that it is better not to confuse them. Thus in trying to get clear about the conceptual features of, for example, education, we should try to set aside our evaluation of various practices. Now it is one thing to say that this distinction is by no means easy to observe and quite another to denounce those who try to observe it as "insincere or naive."[23] This charge connects with the nihilism thesis, I suppose, as follows. If, in practice, we are inevitably prescribing, then we undermine the importance of evaluation when we refuse to come out directly and make substantive recommendations.

On the alleged inevitability of prescription, we are told that "the context, particularly the context in which a philosopher of education in England writes, is one in which education already is presumed to be valued. The philosopher is therefore spelling out the content, or the constituents, of something that is valued."[24] But first, the fact that something *is* valued does not mean that we cannot try to get clearer about what this something involves. And we can do this whether or not we ourselves value that thing. Second, analysis may put us in a better position to evaluate the thing in question, though this is not to say that the analysis is itself prescriptive. Third, when what is valued is set out more clearly, it may in fact no longer appear as valuable as it was first thought to be.[25] Thus the presumption of value may be defeated when the content is spelled out. The common charge of conservatism[26] amounts then to nothing more than a danger to be avoided.

The kind of detachment involved in analysis is, moreover, necessary if we are not to take for granted the establishment norms. For unless we set ourselves to examine what these involve, we shall not be in a position to assess them. There is no question here of abandoning the field of substantive values, simply a matter of trying to be as clear-headed as possible about the recommendations which we wish to make. It is, of course, true that many groups will want to impose their ideologies on others, and not hesitate to ignore, or distort, serious criticisms of their views. But it may also be that the only effective way to counter this is to encourage the development of the critical values in children.

To suspend judgment on an issue until one has tried to gain some understanding of it is not to forsake substantive value questions, but to approach them seriously. Far from annihilating values, we strengthen them by distinguishing them from matters on which one view will do just as well as another. If we adopt open-mindedness as an aim of education, we do not fall into that self-contradiction which, as others have shown, follows from the view that education should be characterized by open-ended questioning.[27] Open-mindedness does not clash with the correct view that "the logic of criticism entails positive assertion,"[28] for, in forming *or* revising our views, open-mindedness can still be preserved, since it can characterize *the way in which these are held.*

REASON AS REMOTE

Yet another aspect of the nebulous concept of detachment prompts the idea that a commitment to the critical values leads to a neglect of one's personal feelings. Mary Warnock has warned us of "the absolutely rational parent observing a child's tantrum and letting him simply go on screaming."[29] The person who is detached is not to be swayed by feeling or emotion, but decides what to do as a result of rational reflection. The problem, then, is that a commitment to a rational approach may drive out that emotional response which is so important a part of a fully human involvement in morality. We can think, for example, of Euthyphro's disturbing indifference to the fact that it is his own father he is prepared to prosecute.[30] There is indeed a twofold problem here. In the first place, we may act as required, but in such a way as to fail to show sympathy or care. Or second, in setting our human feelings aside, we may act, as the Nazis did, in ways which are terribly wrong. This possibility, then, explains the view that "Stalin and Hitler did not need to think harder, but to feel differently about people."[31]

The view expressed here, that what is needed is something other than reason to balance one's judgment, can be buttressed to some extent by the fact that the fanatical person is, as R.M. Hare has put it,[32] unassailable in argument. Given that rational argument is ineffective, it is natural to suggest that we might be more successful if we could communicate with fanatics at the level of ordinary human feelings.

It is easy to show, however, that it is simplistic to conclude that "we should be positively partial to as much as we can."[33] Our feelings *can* lead us astray. Socrates pointed out the danger of being taken in by such appeals as the possible loss of one's friends when one is trying to answer a difficult moral question.[34] He himself refused to engage in emotionally charged pleading with the court, and indicated how this can distort the judicial process. The judge's task is "not to make a present of justice, but to give judgment."[35] To play on feelings is to run the risk of confusing matters, and to lead away from the central question of what it is *right* to do. It is all too easy to allow our feelings to give weight to factors which, in a "cool hour," we can recognize to be irrelevant. The fact that we are often inclined to excuse those whose emotions lead them to act in ways which are morally wrong is an indication of the ease in question.

Is reason then to be seen as in opposition to feelings? Does a rational inquiry dictate a cold indifference to human feelings? Consider again the view that Hitler did not need to think harder, but to feel differently about people. Here the suggestion is that his thinking as such cannot be faulted, yet his actions were morally heinous. In the first place, however, a person may act in such a way because he has closed his mind to what his *own* feelings are. He may seek to avoid situations, as apparently many Nazis did, which will only remind him of those feelings. Here, if the person would only *think about* the consequences of his actions, he would experience the same feelings of disgust as others. In pursuit of an ideal, the fanatic may easily ignore the tremendous sufferings his actions bring about. But once again, the person is not thinking hard enough, for he is not taking all the relevant factors into account.

Second, the fanatic who does not ignore these factors, but nevertheless has no compassion, still comes in for rational criticism, even though he will not be moved by this. Why exactly is it, for example, that a certain skin colour justifies a man being treated in a certain way? The racist has an obligation to show the relevance of the criterion he employs, but this he is unable to do. It is not sufficient to point to *a* difference (*any* difference). The difference has to be such that it warrants differential treatment. Thus, although the fanatic may be "unassailable in argument," it remains true that he is not thinking hard enough, for he is failing to press the question of relevancy seriously enough.

Reason connects with feelings in a third way. We can ask ourselves how *we* would feel if others were to treat us as we treat other people. Here, the opposition built into "not ... to think harder, but to feel differently" is further weakened, because it is through a more serious and imaginative application of the principle of universalizability that we may come to feel differently. We do need to feel differently, but this does not mean thinking less but thinking of things we are at present neglecting. Here again, it is true, but irrelevant, that the appeal to universalizability may achieve nothing. We need to recall that the position being criticized is that Hitler did not need to think harder. We can properly hold that he needed to, even if his fanaticism made it in fact the case that argument would not move him.

Again, it is perfectly possible to ask if our emotional response is at all appropriate in the context in question. Is it, for example, proper that we have no feelings of guilt given what we have done? Is our fear and hatred of blacks or Jews reasonable? We know that the object of fear or hatred may be unsuitable,[36] hence we can ask about the appropriateness of our emotions, and serious thinking here can lead to changes. It is not just any kind of emotional response which is called for, but one which fits the situation. We are in a position to say that Hitler needed to feel differently about people, because the feelings he had were, and can be shown to be, inappropriate. Reason is not remote from this case but has a close bearing on it.

Not only is it possible to ask such questions, it is also necessary if we are to be at all confident that our feelings be directed at appropriate objects. Hence it is important to examine the facts of the case carefully, and be willing to consider what might be said against any position we adopt. In the context of a serious social injustice, for example, it is easy to understand how some can grow impatient with the rational approach, and thus we hear that what we need to do is to become angry and to act. But this, of course, is already to appraise the situation in a certain way, and it is always possible to ask if the appraisal is correct. This question cannot be ruled out of order. It is necessary for it to be raised, unless the appraisals of some are to be taken as authoritative and binding. And it is not difficult to point to important examples, such as the Jensen case, where anger has been misdirected.[37]

It is worth noting here, since it is quite commonly denied, that anger is not a necessary condition of serious criticism. This would seem to be implied by those who have contempt for "polite" commentaries on the work of other people.[38] There is no absolute, indefeasible obligation to be polite, of course, but when we are our criticism may yet be fundamental and telling. We may well judge this to be the most effective way to voice our opinions on matters about which we care deeply. None of this is to deny that there will be many occasions on which it will be perfectly appropriate to become, and to show that one has become, angry.

Finally, we may note that there is no reason to think that a critical approach involves a remoteness from action. We are told, for example, that "it is no good ... thinking that moral education is learning to think critically *about* morals. A person morally educated in this sense might be committed to no moral principles."[39] Now certainly, it is possible for a person to understand what he ought to do, yet fail to do it, or even to try to adopt the principle which enjoins it. And "moral education" might become the name of an examinable subject very far removed from the sphere of moral action.[40] In so far, however, as a person is willing to think critically about morality, there is the possibility of bringing out the point that moral considerations are binding and overriding. It is, incidentally, an oversimplification to say that when one discusses, for example, the nature of moral considerations, "one is no longer talking about moral education but about moral philosophy."[41] The latter is an important aspect of moral education, and serves to emphasize the connection with action. To be seriously asking what one ought to do is to be looking for principles which can guide one's conduct.

CONCLUSION

General agreement about the meaning of open-mindedness has seriously misled various philosophers into thinking either that there is no useful philosophical work to be done in this area, or that one would have to cook up and concoct difficulties. As we have seen in this chapter, however, open-mindedness is directly attacked by philosophers who know what it means but who think its value to be negative or overrated.[42] My purpose here has been to uncover those conceptual confusions which lead to such criticisms being made. The following chapters will illustrate how such mistakes have led to a distrust, or even a rejection, of open-mindedness in a wide variety of contexts.

Our first example comes from the area of elementary education, for here is a case where even those who are generally supportive of open-mindedness as an ideal tend to draw the line. John McPeck no doubt speaks for many when he argues that the schools are already fully and properly occupied in teaching basic information, the latter being necessary before any kind of critical thinking is possible.[43] Against this, however, we may well ask why, if children are thinking at all as they learn basic information and skills, they could not be thinking in an open-minded way about what it is they are learning. And it is not clear why this would take time away from other important tasks. It will be argued here that open-mindedness is not something to be postponed until a later stage when there is more time, but an attitude which can and should be fostered early on so that it becomes part of one's general approach to study. It is vital, therefore, that we examine the reasons which lead people to think that open-mindedness is not appropriate in elementary education.

CHAPTER TWO

Open-mindedness in Elementary Education

Open education has been a fashionable and influential idea in recent years,[1] and the interest here has produced useful work on discovery learning, creativity, learning by experience and growth.[2] As a result, we are much clearer than ever before about the value and limitations of the practices associated with these ideas. The emphasis, however, has been on certain approaches to teaching and methods of inquiry, as the concepts would suggest, rather than on the important matter of one's attitude to knowledge. Given that the open education movement was clearly concerned about authoritarianism in teaching, it is curious that the central concept of open-mindedness should have been all but ignored.[3]

Despite the fact that open-mindedness is a familiar notion, and relatively uncontroversial as a general aim of education, it is worth looking at closely for a number of reasons. In the first place, it is not always carefully distinguished from related ideas such as tolerance and scepticism, with the result that open-mindedness is sometimes thought to involve relativism and the loss of any kind of certainty in the area of knowledge claims. Second, we need to have a more precise understanding of the idea if we are to look seriously for ways in which the attitude might be promoted. What exactly does open-mindedness involve?

Essentially, the open-minded person is one who is able and willing to form an opinion, or revise it, in the light of evidence and argument. It is, therefore, the attitude which strikes at the heart of prejudice, where views are reached prior to, and independent of, a consideration of the available evidence. The standards aimed at are objectivity and impartiality, the pitfalls bias and error.[4] This characterization is sufficient to indicate the contrast with tolerance, for the tolerant person might never subject his own thinking to criticism. Again, we see that scepticism is not implied, because a person may have the utmost confidence in a view which he is nevertheless prepared to revise if counter-evidence should come up. Finally, we may note that open-mindedness does not demand that we be neutral,[5] for we do not cease to be generally open-minded individuals if we remain willing to revise whatever views we have formed. The persistent tendency to identify open-mindedness with neutrality arises, I think, because we commonly say that we are open-minded about some particular issue only when we have not reached any conclusion about it. But this perfectly proper usage should not blind us to the fact that we can remain open-minded about the views that we hold. Here we are speaking of a general trait.

As students become involved with more advanced work, it is not difficult to see how this trait becomes relevant. Issues which are controversial come up and these demand open-mindedness. The student needs to be aware that hypotheses and theories are always in danger of succumbing to counter-evidence. And so on. We may wonder about the possibility of succeeding in the attempt to promote open-mindedness, in the light of what we know about the hidden curriculum and the likelihood of bias, but it would be difficult to view our teaching as educational at all if open-mindedness were totally ignored. But does any of this really apply at the elementary level?

Certainly, respectable philosophers have expressed doubts about this. McCloskey writes: "I question whether a meaningful distinction can be drawn here between education and indoctrination in respect of the child of 12 or less, and in such a way that the liberal can opt for education alone."[6] For the views of professionals involved in teaching, or teacher education, the evidence is only indirect and anecdotal. Certainly, precious little is ever said about the nature and value of this attitude. And the feedback I receive from teachers indicates that, while the ultimate value of the attitude is not questioned, it is simply not regarded as an appropriate aim at the elementary level. This reaction is not at all surprising, for there are several plausible, though ultimately unsatisfactory, objections to such an aim in elementary education. I shall turn immediately to outline possible objections.

OPEN-MINDEDNESS AS PROBLEMATIC

If we are ever to present a sound case for taking open-mindedness seriously at the elementary level, we must first uncover a number of potential difficulties. One serious objection is based on the fact that much of what is taught in elementary school is very well established and noncontroversial. Let us label this the *epistemological* objection because it arises from reflection on the nature of knowledge in this context. That is, the subject matter is, after all, dealt with in an elementary way, in which simple and basic learning is the objective. Where, we might ask, could open-mindedness come in? A second objection, a *logical* objection, can be introduced to buttress the first, for is it not a simple point of logic that if something is to be unlearned, it must first have been learned? Surely a person can only come to reconsider and revise what he or she has previously come to regard as true. Doubt is not basic, but presupposes belief, and there must, therefore, be a prior process of acquiring beliefs before open-mindedness can get off the ground. In another sense of elementary, then, we must first acquire the elements which would make possible open-minded reflection. The point of the logical objection is to remind us of these truisms.

A third difficulty can be located in the *moral* context. It will readily be admitted that the basic moral principles which we learn as children may need to be appropriately qualified as we grow up, and that the kind of moral considerations we can appreciate is subject to development as we mature. But young children are just not capable of grasping the reasons which a more mature person recognizes as justifying an exception to a moral principle. Since serious reflection on moral principles is just not possible, there is obviously no point in urging that elementary teachers try to have their students engage in it. On the other hand, it is not possible to recommend that a completely neutral position be taken by parents and teachers in the interests of open-mindedness. Our actions as parents and teachers will reveal our moral principles; and, even if we could disguise our moral values, no moral agent can be indifferent about his or her moral principles.[7] This is surely part of what is meant by having a moral principle in the first place. Moreover, it is clearly important that young children develop a firm commitment to certain basic moral principles, at least to the extent that they will not casually abandon them.

We may characterize a fourth objection as *psychological*. This is the argument that if potential difficulties in a view or theory were raised for discussion before the students have an opportunity to come to terms with the ideas, the result would be immense confusion. Even at more advanced levels of study, it is often useful to postpone criticisms until one has tried to get an overall view. We need time to digest an idea, to run with it for a while, to see what it involves and amounts to, before we can be ready to consider revising or rejecting it.

The above objections suggest that open-mindedness is neither possible nor desirable in teaching at the elementary level. Let us conclude this review of problems by noting the point that open-mindedness may not be *necessary*. Here, our attention will be drawn to a certain oddity in talk of teaching open-mindedness at this level. Young children simply have not, as yet, come to be blindly committed to particular views. They are eager to learn, and have not closed their minds to other points of view. It is perhaps only in a secondary and derivative sense that young children can be said to be creative and to make discoveries. But in a perfectly straightforward sense, children can be said to be open-minded. If this is correct, why would we need to adopt open-mindedness as an aim?

TOWARDS A RESOLUTION

It is likely that some combination of the foregoing objections explains the neglect of open-mindedness at the elementary level. I wish to argue, however, that the neglect is not justified. Let us admit, for example, that there is simply no room for open-mindedness with respect to some of the basic information conveyed in elementary school. (I postpone until the next section consideration of a radical doubt about this admission.) It does not follow, however, that there is no room for open-mindedness in teaching such truths. In the *Meno*, for example, Socrates is teaching the slave-boy some elementary geometry.[8] Although the truth in question here is one which can be known for certain, open-mindedness enters in because the boy is encouraged to rethink an early view which had seemed to him to be correct. All the relevant evidence is in on the issue, but this does not mean that it must all be presented to the student. Important lessons about open-mindedness can still be taught in the context of such truths, for students can come to see how they had been strongly committed to a false, but attractive, view. The epistemological objection adopts the perspective of the person who already knows the elementary truth, and neglects the perspective of the young inquirer for whom open-mindedness is possible. Discovery learning, which originated in the *Meno*, tacitly recognizes this, though we need to beware of the slide from discovery learning to teacher neutrality. A second danger with the example is that we may begin to see open-mindedness at every turn. For example, in elementary reading, a student will often revise his reading of a word in the light of the later context of the sentence. This is certainly intelligent reading, but the concept of open-mindedness is not really applicable. The reason is surely that there is no suggestion of the student having to give up an idea to which he had become committed.

It is equally important to stress that much of what is taught and learned in elementary school will have to be revised, and some will have to be rejected, later on. The first of these possibilities is very important in this context, because the teaching must of necessity be elementary and therefore simplified. The child will later learn that earlier views fall short of the whole truth. Perhaps the child is introduced to poetry by way of rhyming verse, and may be reluctant to regard blank verse as poetry at all when it is first encountered. Our initial views that art is representational, that stories teach a moral, or that music is simply a matter of melody, will each have to be revised. Ideas turn out to contain hidden complexities as, for example, when we discover that numbers need be neither whole nor positive. Some ideas will simply have to be rejected, since our knowledge of science, geography, history, and other subjects is constantly changing. Open-mindedness is clearly required.

At this point, however, we need to deal with the logical objection mentioned earlier. This argument is seductive because it encourages us to think of open-mindedness as somehow involving belief *and* disbelief at the same time. And this is impossible, because to believe something is to believe that it is true, which is incompatible with disbelief. To make sense of belief coupled with disbelief, we would have to think of an issue where we are, so to speak, in two minds about it. In such a case, it would surely be misleading to say simply that we believe it. Rather, we recognize that there is something to be said for it.

We can, however, answer the logical objection without invoking such cases. The concept of open-mindedness does not mean that what is learned is at the same time unlearned, which would be paradoxical. It means that the student is taught in such a way that he can begin to see views as tentative. He learns that what is believed is held to be true on the basis of evidence, and that the weight of evidence may shift. We cannot sow the seeds of doubt before belief is acquired, but beliefs can be seen in a certain light. This does not mean that the belief must be wavering or hesitant in the sense that the student is not sure what to believe. It is rather to come to appreciate that there may be more to be said on the topic. The view in question is seen as subject to elaboration, and open-mindedness here means being willing to develop one's first ideas.

It is clear that there can be no by-passing the fact of over-simplification at the elementary level. A large and inevitable part of our subsequent education is precisely the process of refining and qualifying of views taken earlier. Our understanding grows out of our participation in this process, and our ability and willingness to take part are essential aspects of becoming an educated person.

Confirmation of the point concerning the development of understanding is documented in the research literature on moral development,[9] which we can briefly allude to in trying to address the third objection set out earlier. Children progress through various stages in their moral thinking, and they cannot arrive at more advanced stages without first thinking in less mature ways. It is, of course, the fact that at an early age children are not capable of grasping the fully moral reasons which support moral judgments, which leads to the charge that early moral instruction must be indoctrination. If true, this would indeed exclude open-mindedness since indoctrination involves coming to hold beliefs in a closed-minded fashion. The charge, however, is premature. First, we need to ask about the long-term aims of teaching if the indoctrination account is to be made to stick. Clearly, children cannot be open-minded about reasons which they cannot comprehend, but they may or may not be encouraged to explore such reasons as they develop. And this would be an important test of the teacher's intentions. Second, taking note of the fact that children can get stuck at lower levels of moral thinking, we can surely claim that that teaching is open-minded which seeks to stimulate and promote the child's development through the stages. It is open-minded precisely because it strives to keep the child's mind open to new ways of thinking about moral issues.

There is, I think, much good sense in the fourth, psychological, reservation. Is it possible, for example, to begin to convey the point about the shifting weight of evidence without making the students more sceptical than we intend? Is it possible to show how initial views must be qualified without suggesting that early learning is trivial? Is it possible to act as an open-minded teacher (admitting, for example, that one is wrong or ignorant) without undermining the trust and confidence which the student has and needs? These questions show the way in which values have to be weighed, and, certainly, open-mindedness is not the only value to be taken into account. It is also clear that we can hardly expect a context-free answer to such questions. The possibilities will depend upon a variety of factors, including the teacher's ability, the students' attitudes, the wider social context, and so on. It is not a failing of psychology that it cannot provide a universal law-like answer to the above questions. What it can try to provide is a fuller understanding of the possible outcomes, and detailed accounts of what is likely in certain sorts of contexts. It is this kind of information which puts the teacher into a position to exercise intelligent judgment in his or her particular teaching context. Since open-mindedness is *one* value, it will be necessary for the teacher to ask how far it is possible to pursue this aim without jeopardizing other valuable aims.

But is it necessary to ask this at all if, as was admitted earlier, young children are not locked into particular views so that their minds are closed? We are now in a better position to appreciate the fallacy which lies behind this tempting line of thought. The assumption at work is that aims are states to be *attained*, and the obvious problem is that the state already exists. What is forgotten, of course, is the way in which aims can refer to states being *maintained*. We know, in fact, that the potential progression through the stages of moral development is not always sustained, and that closed-mindedness can set in. The aim of open-minded teaching at the elementary level is to ensure that this does not occur. We are not teaching open-mindedness in the sense of having our students *become* open-minded for the first time, but rather in the sense of fostering a long-term disposition.

A STRONGER STAND?

It may well be thought that I have missed an obvious way of reinforcing the defence of open-mindedness. Certainly, this will be the view of those teachers who have been influenced by developments in the sociology of knowledge.[10] The charge will be that the epistemological objection has been dealt with far too gently. It is itself epistemologically naive because it misrepresents the character of knowledge. What we "know" is never complete or final, and is always a matter of opinion. This is completely overlooked by the objection which assumes that some knowledge is absolute and certain. In the context of teaching, a typical statement of this sort of radical thesis appears in the following comment on social studies: "In the last analysis, what passes for knowledge is really only interpretation ... A good inquirer knows that what is touted as knowledge-as-fact is only someone's opinion of reality and that opinion is colored by a frame of reference or background of experience unique to the individual."[11] These contemporary views are more extreme versions of theories outlined in older, and more cautious, sociological writings.[12] The attraction is that if we free ourselves from the view that knowledge is more than opinion we will see that open-mindedness is the only sensible attitude to adopt.

Such a thesis is, however, open to a self-referential objection because, on its own argument, the thesis must be nothing more than someone's opinion. It could not claim to tell us anything *true* about knowledge. But even if it were true, it would not serve the cause of open-mindedness. There would seem to be little point, for example, in discarding one view for another which is no closer to the truth. It was for this reason that I was anxious to distinguish open-mindedness from scepticism in the opening section. Open-mindedness does not imply that there is nothing which can be known, but rather that any claim to knowledge can in principle be revised.

In the elementary context, it is immensely implausible to suggest that arithmetic, for example, is just someone's opinion of reality. These matters are known to be true, and we cannot imagine how they might be revised. The way in which words are spelled may change, but we are in no doubt that a particular word is now spelled in a certain way. With respect to a host of elementary matters in history, geography, and science, we have every reason to be confident that our claims to knowledge are well founded.

It might be insisted that in fact we can *imagine* how doubts might be raised against even such apparently certain claims as that $2 + 3 = 5$. Descartes, for example, suggested that our confidence here could be undermined by the hypothesis of the evil demon who uses all his skills to deceive us.[13] Certainly, at the contemplative level, to use Descartes' own way of putting it, this is an interesting possibility. But this is not a reason for presenting such truths as less than certain. The kind of logical possibility suggested in the hypothesis is not one which the elementary student can find meaningful. Since the nature of the doubt cannot be appreciated, we would only introduce a distortion if we were to suggest that such truths were open to revision. A further point is that we are very likely to weaken the significance of open-mindedness if we try to extend the notion to such tenuous cases. It may begin to appear as something trivial, instead of the vital intellectual obligation which it is.

OPEN-MINDEDNESS IN TEACHING

Examining the problematic aspects of open-mindedness carefully, we see that open-mindedness can appear in several forms at the elementary level. We can give the child the chance to think out, or to rethink, his position on an issue about which the adult cannot really be open-minded because it is beyond all reasonable doubt. We can begin to introduce the idea that beliefs are revisable, tentative, and emergent. We can look out for signs that children are ready to question their views and give appropriate encouragement. Given the importance of example in teaching attitudes, teaching should itself be open-minded in the sense that the teacher manifests the attitude. In this way, open-mindedness is implicit in teaching. On occasion, of course, it might have to be implicit in a different way, if the teacher deems it necessary to engage in deliberate bias in order to disturb an air of complacency in the classroom. Presumably, the teacher is counting on the students coming to see through the gesture, and to recognize the real purpose.

Is there a case for more explicit teaching of the attitude? It is not difficult to see why there should be doubts about this and why "teaching by example" is favoured. Oakeshott, for example, thought that "the intellectual virtues may be imparted only by a teacher who really cares about them for their own sake and never stoops to the priggishness of mentioning them."[14] The very real danger is that an artificial and unnatural element will enter in, and teaching will degenerate into preaching. If our work as teachers really is infused with such attitudes, we do not need to talk about them. The limited research evidence suggests that, as one would have suspected, attitudes are not acquired through formal instruction.

The case for *some* explicit consideration, however, is simply that it is possible to misunderstand what is involved in a certain attitude. At the implicit level, one is inferring the attitude from overt behaviour, with the result that it may be confused with some other attitude which is also compatible with that behaviour. This is one reason why open-mindedness is commonly confused with neutrality and doubt. At some stage, it is important to spell out clearly what is involved in the attitude of open-mindedness, and to show how it is different from apparently similar attitudes. Didacticism is avoided because the point of the explicit consideration is not to foster the attitude, but to clarify what is being fostered through example.

There will obviously be limits here in the context of elementary education, but we may well have underestimated the conceptual and reasoning abilities of children.[15] If teachers are themselves clear about the main features of the concept, it ought to be possible to look at particular examples which show the difference between open-mindedness and related ideas and to try to explain the difference. We need to begin with specific cases, but go on if possible to a generalized understanding of the attitude. An educated person should have some idea of what the attitude involves, and this is not the same as being able to recognize particular cases. We often neglect the fact that what sometimes stands in the way of open-mindedness is that we do not properly understand what it is. The foundation of such understanding should be laid in the elementary school.

CONCLUSION

We have seen that open-mindedness can constitute an educational ideal even in the early stages. Let us turn, however, to consider the possibility that children should not be encouraged to be open-minded in certain areas. The most controversial area has been that of moral development, where we encounter the surprising fact that many moral philosophers actually oppose open-mindedness in certain sorts of situations.

There is a sense in which open-mindedness encounters limits in the moral context. We have already noticed in chapter 1 how the claims of open-mindedness might be outweighed by moral considerations in particular contexts.[16] A different point, however, is that certain factors always seem to be relevant in the moral situation even if they are not decisive. The fact that a certain action will cause suffering does not mean that it must not be done, but the fact does need to be taken into account.

McCloskey raises the question, concerning such values as human happiness and respect for persons, "whether we ought to try to leave the child's mind open so that he can rationally reconsider their rightness or wrongness. My basic problem relates to the limited respect in which one can rationally reconsider whether pleasure is a good, suffering an evil, and so on."[17] But a limited respect does not mean an insignificant respect. If there are special or exceptional contexts in which suffering is not to be seen as an evil, then it would seem to be important not to close our minds, or those of our children, to this possibility. As we shall see, however, this view is not shared by certain influential philosophers.

CHAPTER THREE

Open-mindedness and Moral Principles

Many moral philosophers, including those who have thought deeply about moral education, argue in effect for closed-mindedness in certain areas of moral life. This stands in sharp contrast to the generally favourable esteem in which open-mindedness is held, nicely illustrated by the rhetorical way in which one philosopher recently asked: Who could be against open-mindedness?[1] This elliptical question really means to ask how anyone could reasonably be opposed to open-mindedness; and it is rhetorical, because the implication is that once we understand the concept, the question answers itself. The reason here is that this attitude – being willing to form and revise one's views as impartially and so as objectively as possible – is itself a central part of what it means to be reasonable.[2] It can, I think, be further argued that open-mindedness is written into that more restricted and normative use of "education" which we employ to suggest certain standards which learning and schooling can, but do not necessarily, attain. If we would not regard a person as educated in this sense who had no regard for truth, that is, no concern to hold true beliefs and to discard false ones, then we must also ascribe open-mindedness to an educated person. Unless a person is willing to form and revise his views in the manner described above, he will not be thought to have a concern for truth.[3]

Similarly, indoctrination is thought of as a form of miseducation because it involves holding one's views in a dogmatic and closed-minded fashion.[4] Moral philosophers would not endorse Plato's attempt to prevent children from forming "opinions the opposite of those we think they should hold when they grow up."[5] They argue, rather, that children must come to think morally for themselves.[6] This is not to say, of course, that moral instruction is to be abandoned. In the first place, open-mindedness will not be satisfied if leaving children to their own devices simply means that they will come to accept in an uncritical and dogmatic manner the prevailing moral code. Second, moral instruction will not entail indoctrination if the teacher's aim is to bring the child to the point where he can think for himself. And third, instruction can itself be conducted in an open-minded or closed-minded spirit, depending upon the teacher's willingness to entertain objections and criticisms seriously.

If open-mindedness is to be regarded as important in the area of morality, indeed if it is to have application at all, it will be necessary to regard reason and evidence as having a role to play in the justification of moral judgments. If, for example, moral judgments were viewed as mere expressions of likes and dislikes, there would be no room for argument and discussion about them. Thus, there would be no application for the idea of forming and revising a moral view in the light of evidence and argument. A further consequence would be that the idea of moral education would have to abandoned. Without going into the difficult question of how reason and evidence come into the formation and assessment of moral views, I shall assume, along with the moral philosophers in question, that discussion and argument are appropriate in the area of morality.

If then open-mindedness has application in this area, let us try to identify different sorts of cases in which it could come into play, in order to see clearly the kind of case in which there is thought to be an argument in favour of closed-mindedness. Our discussion will have two main concerns. First, to ask if open-mindedness does indeed imply the objectionable consequences suggested. And second, to ask if other arguments against open-mindedness are good ones.

THE PRACTICAL CONTEXT

All of us acquire certain general moral principles in the course of growing up. It is clearly possible to ask if these principles are defensible. Perhaps criticisms are made of these principles from time to time, and we can listen to these and try to evaluate them. We can go further and actively look for difficulties in our own views by thinking of situations which will put them to the test. We can also think about which principles we should teach our children. In short, we need not accept uncritically the principles we have acquired, but can be open-minded about them. R.M. Hare has pointed out that unless those who taught us were archangelic, we cannot assume that the principles we have acquired are faultless. In any case, changing circumstances mean that once-sound principles may need to be revised.[7] Hare stresses, however, that such reconsideration requires leisured thought and "a cool hour."[8] In such circumstances, we can employ what Hare terms "level-2" thinking, where we try to arrive at those highly specific moral principles which a completely adequate knowledge of the facts would warrant. Ideally, it is the thinking of a "fully-informed arch-angelic act-utilitarian."[9] We need not, indeed must not, assume that these notions can ever be satisfied in practice.

The principles arrived at in this way will be, in effect, the standard against which our "level-1" principles are judged. The latter are those general moral principles which we use in practical situations as the principles most likely to lead us to do the morally right action. Not being omniscient, we must settle for the act which our principles indicate as most likely to be morally correct. The principles in question are not mere rules of thumb. They are to be *implanted*, says Hare, with the result that the individual will find it repugnant to break them. Clearly, open-mindedness could have application here also. That is, an individual could consider giving up, in an actual situation, his general commitment to a principle. But should he?

It is here, in the practical context of decision making, that many moral philosophers have defended a view which, it seems to me, amounts to a kind of closed-minded allegiance to our general rules. The classic statement is by G.E. Moore: "... though we may be sure that there are cases where the rule should be broken, we can never know which these cases are, and ought, therefore, never to break it."[10] Even if it should seem to us, in the specific circumstances in which we find ourselves, that it would be better to break the rule, we should never do so. We may, of course, want to recall our doubts later in "a cool hour," and engage in the kind of open-minded reflection discussed above. But in the practical context, we are to set ourselves against this.

This is not to say, however, that in practical contexts there will be no room for open-mindedness if we were to exclude decisions to break general rules. Again, Hare has pointed out that, first, there are cases in which our general moral principles come into conflict.[11] Sometimes, of course, there will be a higher-order principle which we can appeal to, but at other times we may have no choice but to decide what we ought to do as best we can in the circumstances. We may find our-selves in a situation in which we have to deal with such a case, and will be obliged to think out our position. We have the fact of serious disagreement, and the absence of a readily available resolution,[12] and open-minded reflection is an attractive alternative to other, arbitrary ways of reaching a decision.

Hare recognizes a second case where open-mindedness may be justifiable in a practical context, but here we have to proceed cautiously since the case is not quite as clear as the first just outlined. Hare describes the case variously as "such an unusual one that we find ourselves doubting whether the principles were designed to deal with it."[13] Elsewhere, he refers to the kind of situation "in which, though there is no conflict between general principles, there is something highly unusual about the case which prompts the question whether the general principles are really fitted to deal with it."[14] Two sorts of cases come to mind. The first (and this tends to be suggested by the former quotation) is one in which, although there is a well-established general rule to the effect that a certain kind of action is permitted, required, or excluded, it is just not clear whether or not a particular action is of the kind covered by the rule. Perhaps the particular action was not possible, and not even imagined, when the rule was formulated. Here, open-mindedness might involve revising an earlier decision to appeal to a certain rule, not on the grounds that it would be better not to keep the rule on this occasion, but because it now seems that the general rule does not apply here at all. Murder may always be, as Moore puts it,[15] a worse alternative, but there may be disputes about whether or not a certain action involves murder. It is plausible, I think, to read Hare as endorsing open-mindedness in such a case.

The second sort of case, however, which might be suggested by Hare's language, is the one condemned by Moore, in which an individual contemplates making an exception to a generally sound rule in a practical context. Here it is agreed that the rule applies, in the sense that the action in question falls within the scope of the rule; but it is arguable whether or not it applies in the sense that it should *govern* this case. The rule is not "fitted" to deal with the case, because an exception needs to be written into the rule. We admit, that is, that the action involves, let us say, murder, but we argue that in this particular case the action would nevertheless be justified.

R.M. HARE'S AMBIVALENCE

R.M. Hare says explicitly that Moore's "never" is too extreme.[16] (It makes no difference to the interpretation of Hare's judgment here whether we take it to refer to Moore's first use of "never" or to his second in the earlier quotation. If the first is too extreme, then the second, which depends on the first, is also too extreme. This reading then is equivalent to applying the judgment directly to the second "never.") Moore, let us recall, was referring to decisions in practical contexts to break what are known to be generally useful rules. Therefore, it would seem that Hare must be agreeing that there will be

occasions on which such decisions in practical contexts will be justified, and, if so, is defending a measure of open-mindedness even here.
It is important to note here that, if Hare disagrees with Moore, it will
not be enough for him to show, or allow, that cases can be *imagined* in
which it would be better to break the rule. Moore is clearly referring
to the practical situation, and if his view is too extreme, it must
follow that it will be justifiable in some actual situations to decide to
break a moral principle.

Moreover, Hare points out elsewhere,[17] correctly as I believe, that
philosophical argument cannot tell us whether in a particular case
the danger of ignoring relevant features of the situation will be greater
than the danger of distorted calculation if we try to take these features
into account. Both dangers must be admitted, but they will arise in
varying degrees in different cases and there is no general way of
telling, in advance, which danger is going to be greater in particular
cases. (Hare rightly notes that it is not a defect in a philosophical
theory that it cannot provide the answer to nonphilosophical questions.) Again, therefore, it would seem appropriate to be open-minded
about our commitment to general rules.

And yet, Hare argues for a kind of closed-mindedness concerning
the matter of deciding to break rules in practical situations. Regarding
slavery, for example, he writes: "This may explain why I would always
vote for the abolition of slavery, even though I can admit that cases
could be *imagined* in which slavery would do more good than harm,
and even though I am a utilitarian."[18] On torture, he states: "I have no
hesitation at all in saying that police officers, however desperate the
circumstances, ought to make it a matter of principle never even to
contemplate such methods."[19] And again, on the same subject, "it is
very much the best thing if they simply rule it out from their minds."[20]
Now it might be said that such statements are not inconsistent with
Hare's professed disagreement with Moore, for he could claim that
Moore's "never" is too strong and yet hold that *some* of our general
rules should never be broken. This is correct; but then Hare owes us
an explanation why some rules justify an extreme stand when others
do not. It will not do, I think, to say that the rules cited refer to
actions which are normally very wrong indeed, for degrees of wrongness can be balanced by a greater degree of good to be achieved. If, as
Hare says, philosophical argument cannot decide in advance for particular cases, how are we justified in closing our minds in advance to
possibly relevant features or particular situations?

Despite the strong statements quoted above, Hare, it seems, would
like to allow for the possibility of making exceptions to general rules
in practical contexts, even in the case of actions which are normally

very wrong. For example, in the context of a discussion of terrorism, he writes: "And we shall be most likely to do what is right if we stick to the principles, not indeed, as Moore thought, on absolutely all occasions, but at least unless we have a pretty cast-iron reason, based on firm knowledge that the case is an unusual one, for breaking them."[21] On other occasions, he maintains that we should stick to our general principles "unless the situations are very extraordinary"[22] and that such situations are "very rare."[23] But if they exist at all, we need some good reason why we should set ourselves to act as if they did not. The value of open-mindedness is not undermined by their rarity, for a rare and unusual occasion may yet be terribly important.

THE PROVISION FOR EXCEPTIONS

Hare is clearly searching for an acceptable compromise position which avoids Moore's extremism on the one hand, and the foolishness of trying to engage in archangelic thinking on every occasion on the other. But he hesitates to embrace open-mindedness, which he is obliged to accept, I think, if he is to disagree with Moore. He is to some extent influenced by the standard objections, which we shall look at in due course, but in addition he advances certain objections of his own.

For example, Hare rightly points out that "level-1" principles cannot fulfil their intended purpose unless they are limited in specificity (which does not mean that they must be extremely simple). Thus: "... if we are going to learn something from our reflexion on a particular case (at least if we are going to learn something *useful*), the principle that we carry away with us cannot be of unlimited specificity."[24] Let us agree then that there is, as Hare puts it,[25] a psychological limit to the complexity and flexibility of our moral principles. But he dismisses too quickly another possibility which would, I think, satisfy the demands of open-mindedness, namely, "provision for writing in exceptions *ad hoc* when the awkward cases arose."[26] It is beside the point for Hare to go on, as he does, to advise what to do in "more normal cases," for it is the awkward ones we are concerned with. What, however, can be said to offset Hare's evident reluctance to adopt the "provision for writing in exceptions"?

First, there is no implication that the acceptance of such a provision means that in effect the person becomes *unprincipled*.[27] J.L. Mackie is right to observe that "we are rightly sceptical about a man of principle who has a new principle for every case,"[28] but this description simply does not fit the person who is prepared to admit the possibility that on occasion one of his deeply held principles may have to be sacrificed.

Similarly, the provision to make exceptions in awkward cases does not set us on that notorious "slippery slope," an argument which Hare thinks has some force "against the too ready abandonment of accepted general level-1 principles."[29] "Too ready," however, begs the question against the provision, for the expression implies that we really do not hold the principle at all. The person who accepts the provision, however, is simply prepared to consider revising his principle in unusual cases. We will, of course, have to take into account, as best we can, the effect on us of making exceptions and of being prepared to make exceptions.

Second, the provision does not imply that our commitment to the principle is shaky, wavering, or hesitant, as the word "flexibility" might suggest. We may not even be able to imagine a case in which we would be justified in breaking the rule, and yet we may hold it "subject to revision." A common error is to think that open-mindedness implies the absence of confidence in our beliefs.[30] But while the open-minded person must entertain doubts in the sense of listening to the criticisms and objections of others, this does not imply that he must have doubts of his own. There is no logical reason why a person cannot be quite open-minded about a belief or principle to which he tenaciously clings.[31]

Third, there is no conflict between the provision and the view that a good person would simply not think of doing certain things. We would, for example, have no difficulty in reproving someone who was thinking of stealing, in the sense of planning to do it and looking about for an opportunity. But more than this, a good person would not think of it, in the sense that it would not normally occur to him as a possibility. He will have habits and inhibitions which lead him simply to follow the general rule.[32] Hare tries to allow for questioning at the hypothetical or imaginative level and to hold, on the other hand, that "to consider doing such a thing *in practice* would show a corrupt mind."[33] But while the distinction between the speculative and the practical context is a fruitful one, it is not ultimately adequate. Hare himself immediately has to introduce an "unless the situations are very extraordinary" clause.[34] The person who adopts the provision simply recognizes this possibility, however remote, and does not on that account deserve to be called corrupt.

Fourth, the provision to make exceptions does not leave us open to the objection, often raised against act-utilitarianism, that the value of being able to count on people acting in certain ways is lost. Richard B. Brandt notes that "it is important to be able to know in advance what other people will do, partly just for peace of mind, but also for efficient planning ... It is manifestly useful for people to feel bound to do certain things unless there is very pressing reason of public benefit (etc.) to the contrary."[35] But first, Brandt himself here acknowledges the fact that circumstances may arise to justify going against a general rule, and it is just this which open-mindedness recognizes. Second, we can still count on people keeping general rules, for it is only in unexpected circumstances that they will even consider breaking the rule. Again, I think, it is only if we link open-mindedness with hesitancy and doubt that we will conclude that we are uncertain how such a person will behave. An open-minded person, however, is not one who is "ready to deviate from a policy at the drop of a pin."[36] Thus there is no suggestion of unreliability.

Fifth, although Hare has shown, I believe, that highly unusual cases can be excluded when we are *selecting* "level-1" principles, it does not follow that they are to be excluded when we are *employing* these principles in the practical decision-making context. They are excluded when the selection is made because "there will have to be a careful proportioning of the weight to be put upon a particular case to the possibility of its actually occurring in the lives of the people who are to use the principles."[37] We are, after all, trying to identify those principles whose general acceptance is likely to lead to the right decisions in most kinds of cases which we actually encounter in life. For this reason, "fantastic unlikely cases will never be used to turn the scales as between rival general principles for practical use."[38] It would, of course, be foolish to frame general principles for ordinary life with regard to fantastic situations. But the provision to make exceptions does not appeal to unusual cases in the formation of our general principles. It is designed to allow us to deal with unusual cases in the unlikely event that they should arise.

SOME CONFUSIONS ABOUT OPEN-MINDEDNESS

We can agree with R.M. Hare that it would not be sensible to bring up children to engage in "archangelic thinking" each time they have a moral decision to make. It is important to see that open-mindedness about our general principles in actual situations does not support such an absurd policy. Some accounts of open-mindedness might suggest that it is open to an objection, usually advanced against act-utilitarianism, that it entails an excessive and unreasonable attention to each and every situation in order to ensure that it would indeed be better to keep the rule. Whatever the merits of this as an argument against act-utilitarianism, I wish to consider it here in a general way in the context of open-mindedness. For example, Montefiore writes:

To be open-minded is after all to be unremittingly sensitive to the possibility that one may not have succeeded in being as impartial and as objective as one may have intended and hoped; that there may still be new facts to be discovered, old facts whose relevance has yet to be reassessed, new interpretations to be considered of the total situation or of certain aspects of it.[39]

David Bridges comments that the open-minded person "will live in constant awareness of the warning that the closed-mind can achieve invisibly that to which not even an army of public censors could aspire."[40] Such descriptions can readily suggest an oppressive and overwhelming state. We might easily think that open-mindedness succumbs to the following objection, raised by Brandt, to act-utilitarianism:

with our present moral code, I know that at the present moment none of my obligations is undischarged – except for more generous charity – and that I am morally free to be reading a novel. Whereas if I really thought I ought to be doing the most good, I would be inquiring into the circumstances of the men engaged at this moment in cleaning a piece of furniture in my living room.[41]

But open-mindedness does not carry these objectionable consequences. First, as Brandt himself notes elsewhere, "it is sometimes or usually obvious when further reflection would cost more than expectable benefits from it (or the reverse)."[42] We will not find ourselves having to inspect every situation exhaustively. Open-mindedness, secondly, does not imply that we are uncertain whether or not we have discharged our obligations. Any tendency to think that it does results from confusing a willingness to revise one's views with being doubtful about those views. Scientists may be completely confident of claims they make which, they nevertheless allow, are "subject to revision." Third, while we *can* display our open-mindedness by actively seeking out difficulties in our views, this is not a necessary condition of being open-minded. We would, I think, grant that a person was open-minded if he were willing to consider seriously (taking into account the point about expectable benefits) those difficulties which come to his attention. There are some situations, such as those in which the person has good reason to suspect that serious difficulties exist, when some active search will be called for. But not every situation is like this. Probably most situations are not. Naturally, we will want to avoid a life in which, as Feinberg has put it, everything is always "up for grabs."[43] But this need not lead us to adopt a closed-minded attitude towards our general principles in actual situations.

THE RISKS IN BEING
OPEN-MINDED

Even if open-mindedness is properly understood, however, any defence of it has to deal with various arguments regularly employed to show that it is better to stick to our general rules. Many philosophers, for example, appeal to what we might call the *argument from human weakness*. Different aspects of human fallibility are cited, including the danger of special pleading. Again, G.E. Moore is particularly forthright, asserting that "our judgment will generally be biased by the fact that we strongly desire one of the results which we hope to obtain by breaking the rule."[44] This argument, however, only amounts to saying that there is a danger of special pleading, and this cannot be denied. But the argument is open to Hare's objection (notwithstanding that Hare himself makes much of the danger of special pleading) that philosophy cannot tell us that this is the greatest danger in particular cases. In another context,[45] Hare provides the distinction we need to reject extremism here, when he points out that the fact that something is possible (e.g., the use of value-laden language by social scientists) does not show that it is inevitable. There are various strategies we can adopt in order to guard against this danger.[46] One fairly obvious way is utilized, and remarked upon, by Plato when Socrates involves Crito in the discussion of the proposed escape from prison, observing that Crito is not facing imminent execution.[47] We can remind ourselves of the danger in question, and of previous occasions when we have succumbed to it. In these and other ways we may be able to form a reasonable judgment that our decision is not a piece of self-interested rationalization. A different point, but one rarely mentioned in this context, is that sometimes a decision to break a generally useful rule involves a great deal of personal sacrifice. In such cases, the argument from special pleading does not get off the ground.

A closely related objection points to the danger of miscalculation in practical contexts. Moore puts it this way: "... the uncertainty of our knowledge both of effects and of their value, in particular cases, is so great, that it seems doubtful whether the individual's judgement that the effects will probably be good in his case can ever be set against the general probability that that kind of action is wrong."[48] Clearly, however, by the time Moore has drawn the conclusion that a generally useful rule ought always to be observed, he has gone beyond saying that it is doubtful whether the individual should trust his own judgment. We cannot be confident that such doubts could never be resolved. Second, Moore is trading to some extent on the fact that it is one individual's judgment set against a rule which is generally accepted as useful. But though the rule is generally followed, the individual may not be alone in his judgment. He may know that his view that the rule should be broken in this case is widely shared, even though very few people are prepared to break a generally useful rule. In such circumstances, the effect of the individual breaking the rule may be to encourage others to do likewise only in similar cases, and not, as Moore fears, to encourage breaches of the rule in unacceptable circumstances.[49] Of course, the individual needs to take into account the probable effects of his decisions on others, but he may be reasonably certain in some cases that his action in breaking the rule will not encourage wrong action.

The risks involved in deciding to break a general principle must not, and need not, be minimized. There is a presumption against breaking the rule. The point is well made by Brandt: "... a conscientious man will take pains to avoid even the appearance of evil, ... a conscientious man will wish to make substantial allowances for the fact that he is an interested party and might have been influenced by his own preferences in his thinking about his obligations. He will therefore tend to hold himself to the received code when this is to his disadvantage."[50] It is quite correct to say that a good person will have a proper concern for his reputation. But, at the same time, there may be occasions when, as Socrates pointed out,[51] he will have to ignore what people will say and think in order to do the right thing. Furthermore, a tendency to hold oneself to the received code is consistent with being prepared to depart from it in certain circumstances.

Again, the risks may be known to be so great in individual cases that it really would be better to decide to stick to the rule. We may recognize that our ability to make appropriate exceptions in practical contexts is so poor that it would be much better to follow the general rules we have learned. To criticize Hare, who acknowledges that there are different types of people, for holding a view which "seems distastefully Platonic and paternalistic in a democratic age,"[52] strikes me as yet another example of allowing one's preferences to colour one's view of what the facts may be. The important point is this: if, in view of the risks, we set ourselves against open-mindedness in the practical context, we do so not because it is itself immoral or absurd or logically incompatible with other desirable traits, but simply because it will in fact not lead to good results. It can still function as an important ideal in our conception of moral education.

CONCLUSION

The arguments thus far have been mainly defensive, designed to show that open-mindedness does not entail certain consequences as alleged, and that well-known arguments against open-mindedness in this context can be countered. But it may be possible in conclusion to begin to take the offensive and show that the point of view being resisted here itself entails awkward consequences. For example, if we take the view that the consideration of one's general principles in a concrete situation is an indication of a corrupt mind, it would follow that Socrates' inquiry into the proposed escape from prison in the circumstances outlined in the *Crito* was immoral. It is true, but irrelevant, that Socrates concludes that the general rules should be observed. The objection applies to even considering the escape. This is strongly counter-intuitive, because the case is a serious attempt to set aside one's natural bias and to try to determine what one ought to do.

Again, we have to be ready, says Hare, to answer the questions and criticisms of those who say that our general principles are not sound.[53] But such questions and criticisms may arise in practical contexts. If we are to answer them, in a sense other than that of providing rehearsed and ready-made replies, then we will be obliged to pay serious attention to them (assuming that they deserve serious attention), and this will inevitably mean entertaining the possibility of breaking the rule.

Moral philosophers often stress that when individuals who stick to their general principles do what turns out *not* to be the right action (by the standards of archangelic thinking), nevertheless their action is justified because they acted so as to maximize expectable utility.[54] The agent is not blameworthy, even though the action proves not to have been right. The fact is, however, that we do on occasion blame individuals for following what is normally a generally acceptable rule. For example, soldiers should normally follow the orders of their superior officers, and there are good utilitarian reasons for this. But as R.M. Hare has himself noted: "We must never lose sight of the distinction between what we are told to do and what we ought to do. There is a point beyond which we cannot get rid of our own moral responsibilities by laying them on the shoulders of a superior, whether he be a general, priest, or politician, human or divine."[55] We will sometimes want to say that an individual *should have realized* that this was an exceptional situation, and excuses may not be accepted. But then, we cannot encourage people never to break, or consider breaking, generally sound rules. We must, it seems, encourage a firm commitment, coupled with the attitude of open-mindedness. We cannot evade our moral responsibility by invoking a generally sound rule.

Open-mindedness does not entail the unwelcome consequences outlined in contemporary moral philosophy. Careful attention to the concept of open-mindedness serves to undermine such objections. The same strategy is required, as we shall see in the next chapter, if we are to deal with the claim that educational standards conflict with open-minded teaching. A great variety of related, but different, points are run together in this general charge and there is no alternative to a careful and thorough sifting.

CHAPTER FOUR

Standards as a Threat to Open-mindedness

If liberal attitudes in general are in a somewhat unhealthy state of confusion these days, open-mindedness is surely an endangered species. Indeed, its nonexistence has already been declared by those who judge the attitude to be purely mythical. Others take the view that it should not, in any case, be protected, since it only serves to promote unwelcome consequences. I have dealt with these matters earlier,[1] and here I wish to address a different, albeit related, concern. It is often claimed that various practices and phenomena associated with the idea of standards in education threaten the ideal of open-mindedness. This amounts to maintaining that certain aspects of standards are incompatible with open-mindedness in teaching.[2] Confusion is endemic here because the criticism shifts imperceptibly from suggestions of logical incompatibility to allegedly insuperable conflicts in practice. The net result is a growing suspicion that, even if open-mindedness is not entirely imaginary, it is all but impossible to achieve, and there is little point pursuing it. My concern throughout is with conceptual issues, and I will not be trying to settle problems of a practical kind *a priori*. On the other hand, it will not be possible to see these problems in perspective without conceptual clarity. Let us begin by examining the ways in which the incompatibility is thought to arise.

THE THREAT OUTLINED

(a) *Setting standards.* Consider, for example, the movement in recent years to state and to require of every teacher a minimum number of competencies. A teacher's performance, on this view, is to be measured against a given set of standards which define what will be regarded as minimally satisfactory. But then:

By giving at the outset a characterization of the skills required for satisfactory teaching, and then using that list of skills as the basis for preparing teachers, one is training teachers in a set mold ... The role definition given to students of teaching under competency based programs is cut-and-dried and one determined prior to training. Since the role definition is not vague or questionable by the student, the student is not likely to think of the role definition as fluid or changing. Hence competency based programs are likely to maintain the *status quo*.[3]

If neither those who set the standards, nor those to whom they are applied, are encouraged to continue to think about the appropriateness of the standards, the threat to open-mindedness is clear. The matter of revising the standards, or of developing new standards, may not arise at all. Allen T. Pearson notes that there is nothing intrinsically wrong with maintaining the *status quo*. Such a judgment would depend upon *what* is being maintained in maintaining the present situation.[4] The point is well taken, for it is too commonly held that change for its own sake is needed.[5] Granting Pearson's point, we can, nevertheless, immediately evaluate a program negatively if it is true that the student does not think of the role definition of the teacher as, at least potentially, "fluid or changing," for in such a case the definition will be maintained whatever the changing circumstances. Open-mindedness is desirable even if the *status quo* is *now* appropriate, hence our concern about the threat must not be treated lightly.

Similar doubts could obviously be raised about teachers specifying in advance instructional objectives for their students. Leaving aside for the moment any assessment of preactive planning of this kind, it is clear that, for some, it has overshadowed the value of judgment in the practical context, where interactive decisions are made during the lesson: "These latter decisions are made with infinitely less deliberation than preactive decisions. It is with the considered, preactive decisions that we are primarily concerned here; for it is at this level that the instructor can more readily engage in rational decision-making."[6] And fears for open-mindedness in teaching may well increase if instructional objectives are understood to mean "measurable learner behavior changes,"[7] the latter being the dominant interpretation in the past twenty years. In the first place, we may begin to ignore a number of objectives, and even logically necessary criteria of education itself, because these cannot be treated in a quantifiable manner. We must surely be alarmed when we encounter the view that "worthy" is hardly a measurable term.[8] If this is to be eliminated, then the possibility of stating an *educational* objective at all is cast in doubt.[9] Second, we may close our minds to the possibility that what is to be learned could be displayed in behaviours other than those specified in advance. This is not the point that there may, for example, be several different, but equally acceptable, answers to a given problem,[10] but rather the fact that a person's grasp of an idea can be demonstrated in a variety of ways.[11] A related danger is that of thinking that the behaviour specified will show conclusively that the student has learned what was intended.[12] Something as familiar and valuable, then, as a lesson plan may be thought to conflict with an open-minded approach to teaching. The attitudes of the inquiry teacher, we are told, are such that "the only kind of lesson plan, or syllabus, that makes sense to him is one that tries to predict, account for and deal with the authentic responses of learners to a particular problem."[13] Similar fears lie behind Michael F.D. Young's concern about the typical conception of a lesson which involves an attempt "to guide pupils to fit in to the teacher's prior plan of the lesson."[14] Such a conception is contrasted with one which accepts an inbuilt unpredictability of outcomes.

(b) *Assessing standards.* Teachers are also involved in trying to determine whether or not certain standards have been met, and we can use "assessment" as the generic term for a variety of ways of discovering what has been learned.[15] It has long been known, of course, that it is easy to go astray in making such assessments. We have already noticed the way in which a teacher can place too much faith in a particular criterion, assuming that the appearance of a certain behaviour ensures that the student has learned. But this, at least, is a case of a relevant factor being interpreted as a sufficient condition. More disturbing is the fact, detailed in empirical studies, that completely irrelevant factors can influence a teacher's judgment. When students are streamed or tracked, that is, placed in different groups according to their abilities, many factors such as sex, date of birth, and class have been identified as influential in affecting the placement.[16] A recent study in Canada indicates that "physical attractiveness seems to be a criterion which plays an important role in the way in which pupils are evaluated."[17] To make matters worse, it seems that this criterion does not become less influential as student teachers progress through university.[18] If open-mindedness aims at objectivity and impartiality, the ideal seems elusive indeed.

The threat to open-mindedness, however, goes deeper than this. The assessment itself has been shown to have an effect on future performance and assessment. After students have been labelled as academic achievers or as of low ability, actual performance seems to respond to the expectation producing the now infamous self-fulfilling prophecy.[19] Not only does the teacher not expect the low-ability student to do well, there is even some suggestion that the teacher may resent the student's attempt to improve.[20] Thus, although the student may actually improve, the initial assessment can prejudice the teacher's judgment, and adversely affect any subsequent assessment of the student. As Herndon puts it, "in the dumb class he can't learn anything, and there is no reason to expect that he ever will as long as he is in there."[21]

There are other, equally familiar, problems. Creativity, imagination, and independent-mindedness may be overlooked, or even penalized, as the teacher looks for a particular, correct response. And the student in turn learns to supply what is required, as he finds that the school does not appreciate his talents.[22] A teacher's reputation as a tough grader may discourage a student from taking a class which interests him. The result is a scurrying after what Sidney Simon has called, in a depressingly accurate phrase, "snap and crap courses."[23] But then the process is serving to close off a student's developing interests. Finally, to call a somewhat arbitrary halt, we might note the conflict between an open-minded approach to a student's work and the constraints of the "normal curve" which determines in advance that a certain percentage of students must fail. The problems are numerous and the clash with open-mindedness striking. We are bound to wonder if any reconciliation can be effected.

(c) *Maintaining standards.* Typically, schools recognize that an important part of their task is to preserve certain sorts of values, a point illustrated by the aptness of the metaphor of initiation.[24] The standards are to be kept alive by bringing each new generation to share in them. Such a conception has led, not surprisingly, to the charge that education is fundamentally conservative,[25] and in a way which is more pernicious than that implied in the *status quo* objection raised earlier. There, at least, standards were being decided on, but here they are merely being inherited. Hence the charge that they are simply *taken for granted.* Let us see in more detail the forms which such alleged conservatism might take.

First, within subjects or fields, certain traditional norms are allowed to dominate. Thus the standards of "standard English" are imposed on the child who comes to school speaking a dialect which may be rich and effective. Second, between subjects, accepted conceptions of the nature of the disciplines establish firm boundaries. Certain questions are ruled out of order as being irrelevant, because they belong elsewhere. Third, between the subjects of the school curriculum and those which are omitted, a gulf emerges which reinforces the view that only what is learned in school is worth learning.[26] Fourth, within the curriculum itself, a hierarchy develops which places the value of academic courses above those of practical subjects. And the very divisions reinforce the view that there are experts in these specialised areas whose authority must be respected.

Behind these specific points lies the general criticism that, in maintaining standards, the school has become an instrument of middle-class domination. Language itself is infested with bourgeois values making it difficult even to articulate alternative points of view. The result is that even if teachers, inspired by sociology, adopt strategies designed to avoid imposing accepted norms, the reality is that "such notions are sustained by a whole variety of more or less subtle means."[27] Fundamental change in our approach to school subjects is "likely to be impossible in our society."[28]

At a more mundane level, we may note finally that the notion of "maintaining standards" sometimes comes to mean having a deliberate policy of a high failure rate in one's classes. It will not do to be perceived by colleagues as running easy courses: "On our first visits, the faculty in the supposedly softer fields, such as education and sociology, assured us that they were as tough and flunked as many students as their colleagues in other fields."[29] We return then to the problems associated with setting and assessing standards. The teacher's concern to be perceived as preserving high standards interferes with any open-minded consideration of the goals which it is reasonable to set, and also affects his judgment whether or not they have been met. The way in which the issues overlap here remind us that the divisions employed are, in part, just a convenient way of organizing the problems. These have been allowed to mount up without comment precisely in order to convey the way in which such a cumulative effect can undermine our confidence in the feasibility of this ideal. It is time, however, to assess the overall effect by looking in turn at the individual points.

THE THREAT CONTAINED

There is no possibility of removing the alleged incompatibility between standards and open-mindedness by simply removing one of these criteria. The notion of standards is central to any concern with education, for an experience is educational or educative only if certain norms are satisfied. Even if we exclude this point about the normative character of education, it will remain true that, in teaching any subject, some things will count as succeeding in that endeavour and other things will not. This is a condition of intelligibility, for without it we would have no coherent idea of what the subject involved. We cannot, on the other hand, eliminate the concept of open-mindedness, because this is one of the standards built into our concept of education.[30] There is no alternative but to deal with the various difficulties to see if the criteria can be reconciled.

(a) *Objectives.* The first distinction we require is surely that between a view and an inflexible view. The very notion of "setting," with the connotation of hardening which comes across in Pearson's reference to a "set mold," blurs this vital distinction. To establish an objective is not, in itself, to preclude further consideration of that objective. Moreover, it is not necessary to couch the objective in vague language in order to permit open-minded reflection. This may indeed make it more difficult to consider the objective. Phrases such as "cut-and-dried" when applied to role definitions are misleading because they tend to suggest that there is nothing more to be said. But this suggestion is not contained in the idea of a precisely stated objective. The general point is that the language we use to characterize the nature and fixing of objectives can function so as to limit our perception of possible changes. But neutral language is available and question-begging descriptions can be avoided. The distinction mentioned above, which is in danger of being ignored, is one to which the attention of student teachers can, and should, be drawn.

The points made above will also be relevant to the situation in which the teacher sets instructional objectives, but further instances of confusion require additional attention. For example, the importance of open-mindedness at the interactive level can be neglected if we identify rational decision-making with lengthy deliberation. We may see at once in practice that an objective which had been given careful consideration simply cannot be achieved in the circumstances, and a more sensible alternative may immediately present itself. A teacher will, of course, have to develop a sense of judgment about this, but at least we should not be saddled *a priori* with the view that on-the-spot judgments fall short of rational decision-making. This kind of flexibility, favoured by those such as Young who want to preserve an element of unpredictability, is not in any serious way at odds with the idea of a lesson plan. There is no conceptual problem with the notion of a tentative or revisable plan. And we need not hesitate to speak of planning to abandon our lesson plan if that proves to be necessary, because this is simply to plan to teach with an open mind. Moreover, there is nothing sinister about the teacher having a predetermined goal, despite the pejorative tone of having the pupils "fit in" to the plan. Closed-mindedness is not revealed in having an objective as such, but by the way in which the objective is pursued. If the teacher is willing to take into account such things as the criticisms raised by students, there is no reason why a teacher could not have a predetermined objective *and* deal with the "authentic responses" of the students.

Our attitude towards objectives in general needs to be carefully distinguished from our attitude towards certain sorts of objectives. There is, for example, an important sense in which Ralph Tyler was right in insisting that intelligent reflection on educational programs means that "we must first be sure as to the educational objectives aimed at."[31] We cannot, in other words, make sensible decisions about methods, content, and organization unless we have some idea where we are headed. In the absence of this, what would count as making a poor choice? The importance of attending to the distinction drawn at the beginning of this paragraph is shown clearly in the following comment on Tyler:

Recently there have appeared some published doubts, questions, and criticisms of the value and use of the Tyler rationale and, in particular, the primacy of objectives. For example, there arises the valid point that the stating of objectives in specific and simple behavioral terms (as advocated by the Tyler people) does indeed restrict the curriculum. Their specificity can limit teachers who are generally interested in broad changes so as to maintain curricular flexibility.[32]

The obvious reply to this is simply that if there are objections to certain sorts of goals, this is in no way a criticism of the view which recognizes the primacy of objectives. This latter view has to be taken as a logical claim, and not misunderstood to mean that objectives are more important than other considerations. It is clear that one's objectives may have to be revised or rejected in the light of possibilities in the teaching context. Finally, we should note that it is not the fact that an objective is made specific which introduces inflexibility. It is rather our attitude towards that objective. As we noticed earlier in the discussion of vague language, specificity may make defects that much easier to detect.

Of course, if specificity means that only one kind of objective, such as a behavioural change, will be regarded as suitable, then we are in danger of neglecting altogether other important goals. We have already seen how value terms such as "worthy" can be regarded as inappropriate. And it will not do to suggest that such terms could be translated into behavioural language: "... an agreement could be reached that one of the elements of worthy use of leisure time is interest and proficiency in one or more follow-up recreational activities ... Inventories exist that can be used to measure interest, and proficiency can be measured against performance criteria."[33] We can always ask, however, of any proposed definition of a value term if the thing in question really is valuable, and the definition then must remain open to ongoing examination. Open-mindedness requires that we be willing to go on asking if allegedly worthy activities *really are worthy*. This is not to say that all such definitions are useless, only that they do not succeed in closing off the value question. Again, as the points raised earlier indicate, we need to ask if the inventories have managed to capture all the ways in which interest can be manifested, and if they invariably show that the student has interest. We need to remember that many important educational goals, when translated into behavioural terms, can only be indicated by a range of behaviours which are typical but not invariable. This would certainly be true, for example, of traits of character and intellect.[34] Behavioural objectives can be helpful in eliminating hopeless confusion and intolerable vagueness and, if treated as tentative rather than final, relevant but not conclusive, they need not constitute a threat to open-minded teaching. What is true, however, is that proponents of behavioural objectives have not been enthusiastic about open-mindedness. This point can be appreciated if we turn our attention to the second aspect of standards.

(b) *Evaluation.* The discussion of behavioural objectives has reintroduced the matter of assessment because the point has been made that the teacher will need to conduct an ongoing evaluation of the objectives which were set. For one thing, unexpected developments may occur. Popham comments as follows: "We should judge an instructional sequence not only by whether it attains its prespecified objectives, but also by any unforeseen consequences it produces. But what can you tell the would-be curriculum evaluator regarding this problem? "Keep your eyes open" doesn't seem to pack the desired punch. Yet, it's about all you can say."[35] Lawrence Stenhouse thinks that this admission reveals serious problems in the objectives approach because "an adequate theory should be advancing our knowledge of the situation so that unanticipated results become susceptible to anticipation."[36] This is an odd criticism to make because Popham himself points out in the same context that it is important to try to anticipate ways in which the instructional plan may misfire.[37] And there is no reason to believe that an objectives approach must in principle fail to deal with the problem of the unexpected outcome. Of course, the approach will very likely fail in practice if we follow Popham in belittling the crucial advice to "keep your eyes open." If we ask why this advice seems inadequate, the question-begging nature of Popham's comments becomes clear. It is because the advice is imprecise and vague from a behavioural standpoint that it is found wanting. If we are not, however, already locked into behavioural ideology, we can see that it is excellent advice. We pursue the objective set in an alert and intelligent manner, ready to change course if the situation proves to be counter-productive. Of course, Popham has exaggerated in claiming that this is *all* one can say by way of advice. The *kinds* of things one needs to be on the look out for can be discussed and so on. Popham has little time for this sort of reflection, and suggests that "if there is reason to believe that a particular outcome may result from an instructional sequence, it should be built into the set of objectives for the sequence."[38] First, however, this suggestion simply cannot deal with the problem of the genuinely unexpected development. Second, if our statement of objectives is to be manageable in practice, we will not be able to build every contingency into it. We simply have to remain open-minded as we teach, ready to use our judgment as and when necessary.[39]

The fact that a teacher has prespecified objectives does not mean that creativity must be ignored in education. It is going too far to say, as Stenhouse does, that the objectives approach "mistakes the nature of knowledge."[40] The claim is based on the obviously correct point that a person with knowledge may be capable of thinking in creative and individual ways. But to have objectives is not to ignore the possibility that our evaluation will uncover new insights. Here we will not be able to appeal simply to the established standards in making our assessment, for new standards are in the process of being recognized. There is an important sense in which, at certain levels of education, one of our standards in assessing a piece of work might be that the work should set some new standards.[41]

The difficulties involved in assessing genuinely creative work bring to mind the points raised earlier about the various ways in which assessment can be distorted. Certainly, if we are anxious to aim at impartiality and objectivity in our assessments, we need to take seriously the operation of irrelevant factors. But in discovering these, we are at the same time discovering where our practice needs attention. The findings need not generate a sense of hopelessness, but can suggest how we may guard against such pitfalls. When we become aware, for example, that our judgment can be influenced by physical attractiveness, we are at once in a position to set about trying to counteract this. This is surely one lesson to be learned from the injunction to "know thyself."

Similarly, if we are aware of the phenomenon of the self-fulfilling prophecy, it may be possible to introduce checks which would offset this. Indeed, we can turn the prophecy against the pessimistic view, for if we expect that nothing can be done to avoid distortion in assessment, presumably nothing will be done. This is not, of course, to argue that something can be done just because we think it can be done, but to abandon the prejudice that distortion is inevitable.

It must surely be beyond dispute that there can be serious objections to the ways in which assessment is sometimes carried out, and to the uses to which labels deriving from assessment are sometimes put. If, to put it bluntly, we brand a student "slow-learner," we may be ensuring future failure for teacher and student. It is vital, however, to recognize that these objections do not constitute a case against assessment itself. Assessment in some form is necessary if we are to determine whether or not our teaching has been successful, and we cannot be serious about teaching if we are not concerned to discover this.[42] And though we are assessing our teaching, the student's performance is also inevitably assessed. Even if the student has not learned because the teaching was poor, the fact remains that he has not learned. The need for assessment, however, clearly does not mean that it must be public or final. Labelling in the pejorative sense is not inevitable, and is quite distinct from assessment itself. It is important to be clear about this, for if confusion leads us to abandon assessment, the notion of being open-minded about our teaching would vanish. We would have given up the only way in which we can sensibly decide to revise our approach.

It is obviously important to be aware of the two extremes of unreasonably high standards and no standards at all, but it is no help to be told that we must simply get the issue of assessment behind us. Standards are necessary, and it follows that it is quite possible that some will fall short of them. John Holt takes the view that "if a student spends a year in my class and learns *something*, then I have no right to fail him."[43] But the ambiguity here cannot be missed. Nobody will quarrel with the view that we must not let our students down, but we cannot allow this connotation to blind us to the fact that a student may fail to meet the appropriate standard. This may happen although we have done all that could reasonably have been expected in the circumstances. It is possible, of course, to be so influenced by such phenomena as the normal curve of distribution that one denies in advance the possibility that all the students may reach a certain standard. Fears for our reputations may encourage this. On the other hand, the phenomenon may only serve to remind us to ask on occasion if our assessment is accurate. The point is that we do not have to interpret the phenomenon as indicating what we *must* find, but only what we *often* find. If it really is a typical finding, and one which is not itself the result of prejudice, then it cannot be dismissed as utterly irrelevant. But it is not decisive in the sense that we can *prescribe* the outcome.[44] If economic or other factors require that only a certain percentage of students can "pass," we simply need to recognise that that aspect of the outcome is determined. This in itself does not mean that the comparative ranking is inaccurate. We clearly need to remain alert to the possibility that the alleged necessities here are in reality artificial ways of maintaining standards.

(c) *Traditions.* In turning to the question of preserving certain traditional standards, we can begin by recognizing that when these are accepted, it by no means follows that they are blindly inherited. Phrases such as "taken for granted" and "given and necessary," which are the stock-in-trade of contemporary sociologists, are simply question-begging in this context. There is no reason why we cannot decide that certain traditional standards continue to be important. If it is thought to be suspicious that our arguments just happen to support traditional standards, that is *all* it is. Even if the arguments were no more than convenient rationalizations, this would not show that the standards in question were not worth preserving. Such standards can, of course, outlive their usefulness,[45] but it needs to be shown, not merely asserted, that this has happened. The possibility amounts to an occupational hazard for the curriculum planner, but this does not destroy open-mindedness. It shows, rather, that it is necessary.

We will immediately be reminded that any attempt at open-mindedness with respect, for example, to prevailing notions of "school" and "knowledge," is likely to be undermined by "a whole variety of more or less subtle means." The problem in dealing with this intolerably vague charge is simply that unless these means are spelled out it is impossible to say how serious the threat is. This elementary point is rarely made because the rhetoric involved manages to suggest that one would have to be somewhat naive to request further information. In the absence of such details, however, we have no reason to give up on open-mindedness. When, on the basis of such charges, we encounter the view that significant educational changes are likely to be impossible *in our society,*[46] we may be forgiven for harbouring suspicions of our own. Our usual scepticism about appeals to undocumented, personal observations of classroom practice is bound to be magnified when we read that "it may also be that knowledge produced in the context of capitalist relations of production will continue to be perceived by many in a manner difficult to transcend: as external and oppressive rather than 'truly human' and liberating, even when (at the analytic level) its categories have been recognised as human products and not natural ones."[47] It is not surprising that observation fails to reveal openness, if this is only to be "truly" found in a different social order.

The point of these remarks is not to deny the existence of subtle forces counteracting sincere efforts to be open-minded in teaching. We have detected some, and there are very likely others. There is no reason to assume, however, that these will present insuperable difficulties. Certainly, those now identified present serious challenges. We may perhaps use the phrase "the hidden curriculum" for such influences, for at one level we can take this to refer to any message conveyed covertly. Barrow is surely right to insist that "there is indubitably a hidden curriculum,"[48] but it is not necessary to agree with Illich that the message is unalterable. That is, it is one thing to admit that a hidden curriculum will be inevitable, in the sense that our actions will be open to other interpretations, and quite another to claim that open-mindedness is thereby lost. There is, no doubt, the permanent possibility of concluding that only what is learned in school is worth learning, that certain divisions or distinctions are beyond question, or that we can only learn when taught by experts, but none of this is inevitable. Our ability to state these dangers is proof that they can be recognized, and we can look for ways in which they can be brought into the open and considered.

Many of the lessons which are implicit in our teaching do not need to be removed, but simply revealed, so that students can consider what it is they are coming to accept. Criteria of relevance, importance, and truth need to be examined not expunged. If they are confused, inadequate, or biased, let this be shown. If curricular changes really are superficial,[49] with the result that traditional standards go unrevised when they are deficient, then the superficiality must be exposed and new alternatives considered. But open-mindedness does not require that we abandon all attempts to defend standards. It requires that we be willing to revise or reject such standards if they fail to withstand scrutiny. If, for example, we find that school knowledge is presented as a commodity, prepackaged by experts for uncritical consumers, this conception must be rejected.

Contemporary sociologists have identified a wider "culture of positivism" which "operates with a notion of valid knowledge detached from particular knowing subjects, and views school knowledge as (at least potentially) verifiable 'knowledge' about a 'real world' rather than arbitrarily legitimated ways of seeing."[50] But here we have a move which is dramatically different from the criticism of knowledge as a commodity. The fashionable cliché that knowledge is not ultimately independent of the knower certainly serves to draw attention to the fact, neglected in the commodity conception, that a person who is said to know that something is the case must be able to show that he *understands* by producing suitable supporting reasons. We are not, however, entitled to ignore the equally central point that what the person is said to know must be true. And we do not settle this question simply by consulting our beliefs. The quotation marks around "knowledge" and "real world" presumably suggest that these notions are spurious, but we are given no reason whatever to accept this suggestion. We cannot accept it if we are to make sense of the person as knower, or if the concept of open-mindedness is to have any force. In rejecting the suggestion, we recognize that our claims to knowledge must meet certain objective standards.

We need not dispute Whitty's point that the very language we use to capture alternatives may serve to maintain the categories we want to challenge, though there is no need to herald this as a Marxist perspective. It is a familiar enough point in the history of philosophy. Hume, for example, notes some of the traps in his discussion of causality.[51] But these can be identified and neutralized if we are persistent and careful. We recognize the snare by actually describing it, in which case there can be no impossibility stemming from the language itself. *Ab esse ad posse valet consequentia.* To show, for example, how the word "pupil" could reinforce the view that one learns from a teacher, is at the same time to formulate a possible alternative. There are, no doubt, many such traps which have not been identified, but there could be no argument to show that these *must* elude us. By the nature of the case, it would be impossible to point to an example.

CONCLUSION

Conceptual confusion lies behind the view that standards in education must eliminate open-mindedness in teaching. How successful we can be in surmounting the difficulties can only be discovered in practice, but there is no reason to judge *a priori* that the effort is not worth making. Perhaps the position defended here will be labelled "possibilitarian," but this is no hardship as long as language is not being manipulated in order to suggest that the position is doctrinal. The possibility in question, of course, is not that of adopting a political commitment, for this is not the only way in which perceived reality can be actively challenged. It is, rather, the possibility of an open-minded commitment to educational standards.

The matter of standards also enters into the fashionable view which we must now deal with. It is commonly alleged that the activity of teaching itself excludes the possibility of open-mindedness. The feeling is that certain assumptions, standards, or concepts are built into the nature of teaching, and these destroy any pretensions to open-mindedness. The merits of this view will be assessed in the next chapter.

CHAPTER FIVE

Open-mindedness and Teaching

INTRODUCTION

Educational theorists have long debated the respective merits of different methods of teaching as ways of fostering open-mindedness. These empirical disputes have had conceptual aspects, for particular methods have been labelled open-minded or closed-minded *per se*.[1] In recent years, however, a much more fundamental and pervasive doubt has begun to emerge in the suggestion that the very act or process of teaching, quite apart from the particular form it may take, strikes at the heart of open-mindedness. The suggestion comes through in talk of passivity, conformity, hegemony, compliance, legitimation, incorporation, and a host of other notions which indicate how thinking is controlled, channelled, and curtailed in the teaching process. In such circumstances, the possibility of open-mindedness is placed in doubt.

Logical difficulties in the idea of teaching at all go back to the origins of the philosophy of education in the work of Socrates.[2] On the face of it, however, the specific incompatibility alleged in recent discussions seems unlikely. The debates about methods of teaching mentioned above in themselves imply that it is at least believed quite generally that teaching and open-mindedness *are* compatible. There does not seem to be any contradiction in the idea of teaching for open-mindedness as there is, for example, an obvious contradiction in teaching someone what that person already knows. Are there not even examples of individuals we would properly want to characterize as open-minded teachers? These considerations cannot be decisive, however, for the beliefs and assumptions may be false. That we are prepared to speak in a certain way cannot show that we are justified in speaking that way. The relative difference between the teacher we call open-minded and the one we label closed-minded may be undermined by considerations which show that the difference is trivial and superficial because any significant degree of open-mindedness is ruled out.[3] In trusting to our common-sense notions, we may only be serving to confirm the pervasive influence of hegemony which prevents us from entertaining the possibility that our common-sense beliefs are mistaken. We do, however, rightly demand an argument before well-entrenched beliefs are discarded, unless our own open-mindedness is to turn, weather-vane fashion, into empty-mindedness. What would such an argument be like?

THE PARADOX OF TEACHING

There is not, in fact, one unique argument at work, but a family network of considerations advanced by a great number of educational theorists who by no means form a single school of thought. Collectively, the arguments present a formidable position. The first task is to understand the nature of the alleged contradiction in linking teaching and open-mindedness. Rachel Sharp has captured an important strand which runs through a variety of objections in the paradox that "before any teaching takes place at all we are taught what to be taught entails."[4] If we ask what being taught entails, the implicit lesson in *any* lesson is revealed. The teacher and student stand in a relationship of authority and deference, and the process of teaching legitimates and reinforces this idea. The relationship in question is, in a way, conceptually necessary. If a person cannot speak at all authoritatively, he or she simply has nothing to teach, and is not a teacher at all; and if a person is not giving consideration to the ideas presented, he or she is not studying with that person. These conceptual truths indicate that here, at least, we do find a hidden curriculum which is unalterable and everywhere the same.[5] Moreover, the lesson is embedded in practice, where the demands, the standards, the routines, the subject divisions, and the stratification of knowledge, which characterize the teaching process, all serve to create a powerful practical ideology.

Similarly, a contradiction in the idea of teaching for critical development is located by Pierre Bourdieu and Jean-Claude Passeron in the very business of pedagogic action:

The mere fact of transmitting a message within a relation of pedagogic communication implies and imposes a social definition (and the more institutionalized the relation, the more explicit and codified the definition) of what merits transmission, the code in which the message is to be transmitted, the persons entitled to transmit it or, better, impose its reception, the persons worthy of receiving it and consequently obliged to receive it and, finally, the mode of imposition and inculcation of the message which confers on the information transmitted its legitimacy and thereby its full meaning.[6]

The connection between teaching and imposition is in fact expressed in a universal proposition about all pedagogic action.[7] It is hard to see how, on this view, one could escape the conclusion that teaching and open-mindedness are just incompatible. Teaching must, after all, somehow involve the transmission of a message, and it is this which leads to the charge of imposition.

If we are tempted to find openness in project work, discovery learning, and participation in laboratory experiments, Michael Young reminds us that "doing becomes equated with following worksheet instructions *for doing* and the emphasis on resources implies the teacher as initiator of activities."[8] The teaching of science distorts that subject in various ways, reinforcing an arbitrary division between academic and nonacademic science and between science and technology. It cannot but suggest that science is a body of knowledge to be mastered. The pupil cannot be recognized as a scientific theorist in his own right. Scientific knowledge comes to be viewed as a commodity and in this way the very nature of science is distorted, and arbitrary constraints are placed on questioning.[9]

The argument from the paradox of teaching is not, however, confined to those writing from an avowedly Marxist perspective. A similar point emerges when it is claimed that the sex of the teacher is a relevant qualification or disqualification for teaching courses in women's studies.[10] No matter how sympathetic, open-minded, or fair the male instructor may attempt to be in dealing with feminism, the hierarchical relationship between teacher and student reinforces this same relationship between the sexes when the teacher is male and the students female. Such a situation "exhibits a contradiction between the form and the content of what is being taught ... through the very structure of the situation, those traditional sex stereotypes are being reinforced."[11] The argument speaks of a "contradiction," and the problem is described as inescapable, at least in any world in which courses in women's studies are needed. The supporting language, and the general nature of the argument itself, make it clear that we are not being informed of difficulties which practice might resolve. The problem is built into the teaching relationship.

Other writers discover the paradoxical nature of teaching when that process occurs in the context of compulsory schooling. Edgar Z. Friedenberg, for example, is quite explicitly trying to establish a more fundamental objection than that which sees schooling as a mechanism for perpetuating a class-stratified society, and he calls attention to "the metaphysical absurdity of assuming that experience can be handled this way at all."[12] Teaching in school necessarily distorts the nature of human experience, since it forces students to attend only to what has been arranged, and to learn "not just the right answers, but the only possible questions."[13] Elsewhere, Friedenberg appeals to the concept of hegemony to suggest how the distortion is protected from critical examination, for values and categories can only be examined on their own terms.[14] Teaching defines the limits of the questions with the result that other important questions are simply ignored.

Philosophers of education have also sensed a conflict between teaching and open-mindedness. One argument here points to the assumptions which are inevitably involved when we teach anything. Even if teaching takes the form of raising questions, those very questions rest on certain assumptions: "Like it or not, educating involves and requires certain axioms, definitions and other assumed truths. Everything cannot be open to question. If it were, there would be no standards by which we could evaluate the alternatives nor any bases for drawing conclusions."[15] A related second argument finds the notion of teaching rationality incoherent, when teaching connotes rational persuasion rather than indoctrination: "... rational persuasion will work only if one already has accepted and believes in the value of rationality ... it is actually impossible for the students to question the value of developing and using their rational capacities."[16] It is impossible to be open-minded about open-mindedness itself, and, therefore, teaching in this context cannot itself be open-minded. It cannot take the form of an open-minded inquiry into the value of the attitude in question.

Perhaps the *locus classicus* of doubts about the viability of a distinction between teaching and indoctrination is the now infamous claim that "every educational institution makes use of indoctrination. Children are indoctrinated with the multiplication table; they are indoctrinated with love of country; they are indoctrinated with the principles of chemistry and physics and mathematics and biology, and nobody finds fault with indoctrination in these fields."[17] Even sophisticated writers like Kohlberg tend to run the concepts of teaching and indoctrination together: "... the experiences by which children naturally move from stage to stage are non-indoctrinative, that is, they are not experiences of being taught and internalizing specific content."[18] It is worth noting too that many who in general would draw a distinction think that the concepts cannot be distinguished at the earlier levels of education.[19]

Even when the paradox of teaching is not explicitly described, there is a good deal of indirect evidence that something of a contradiction is sensed. It is a remarkable fact, for example, that in the general literature on open education, there is a marked preference for such concepts as guiding, stimulating, mediating, facilitating, discovery, being a resource person, and so on, over such concepts as teaching and teacher. The implicit suggestion is that a conceptual reordering is required if we are to make sense of openness in education. Something quite similar can even be detected in certain historical philosophers, such as Socrates and Descartes, who strongly favoured open inquiry. Both were anxious to make it clear that they were not teachers.[20]

It has sometimes been claimed, notably by Israel Scheffler,[21] that the concept of teaching implies an attempt to promote learning in such a manner that the student's intellectual integrity and judgment is respected. The paradox of teaching not only rejects this as an analysis of the concept, but claims also that it contains an ideal which cannot be realized if it is taken as a stipulation. We only fabricate a concept which cannot be satisfied in practice. Must we accept this dismal conclusion?

THE POSSIBILITIES IN TEACHING

We may begin by accepting that, in addition to the overt curriculum which teaches the various skills and values and ways of thinking deemed important, there is a further set of values and beliefs being subtly reinforced. It is foolish to deny that such a phenomenon exists, though we may properly question the alleged content of this hidden curriculum. It is sometimes claimed, as we have seen, that the content is always and everywhere the same. Behaviour, however, can be interpreted in various ways, and it is hard to see why interpretations would not vary from one context to another. It is also claimed that the alleged content is unalterable, but this is a mere assertion. No reason is ever offered to support this dramatic charge. No doubt, it is an exaggerated statement of the view that certain interpretations are probable, but in this case it makes sense to work at reducing the probability.

One way of doing this is to turn the phenomenon to advantage, and it is not clear how the radical critics could, on their own view, deny this possibility. Teachers can try to ensure that their own behaviour as teachers suggests that they recognize their own fallibility and limitations. Here the hidden curriculum is one which suggests the importance of inquiry, criticism, and reflection. If it is true that messages are implicit in what we do, as it surely is, then we can attempt to make sure that educationally sound ideas are suggested. We do not need to claim that success is assured, but the charge is that we *must* fail. Here we are owed an explanation. Why is it that the hidden curriculum can only convey certain ideas and not others? It is surely possible for valuable ideas to be picked up in this indirect manner, and there is even reason to think that some such ideas cannot be effectively taught in a direct fashion.[22] Nevertheless, students can be encouraged, directly and indirectly, to reflect on the values and beliefs they are acquiring, so that the danger of unthinking commitment is minimized.

If, on the other hand, the student is learning the sort of content decried by Illich, why can this not become the subject of explicit consideration in the overt curriculum? Perhaps the teacher has inadvertently conveyed a certain lesson, but a change in the teacher's behaviour may prevent such a lesson in the future. It would be a curious theory of education which held that teachers could not learn from their mistakes. Again, the teacher may be able to show that there is a more plausible, and less objectionable, interpretation to be placed on his or her behaviour. But here we may expect to be told that any such explicit consideration will occur in the context of authority and deference, a relationship which undermines the intended lesson.

The threat to open-mindedness only arises, however, if the teacher's authority is taken to imply authoritarianism, and the student's deference comes to mean passive acquiescence. It is one thing to hold that authority and deference are present in the teaching context, for the reasons given in the previous section, but quite another to agree that these concepts imply the further concepts which threaten open-mindedness. Authority itself is not incompatible with open-mindedness, since rational authority derives from knowledge and claims to knowledge can be challenged. Deference, in the sense of giving consideration to the ideas of the teacher, is also quite compatible with open-mindedness. Indeed, we can only form or revise a view in an open-minded way after giving it some consideration. It is only conceptual sloppiness which persuades us that authoritarianism and uncritical acceptance are involved. These may or may not be present, but their presence cannot be inferred from the relationship in question. When it is said that authoritarianism is embedded in a hundred and one routines and practices in school, this might mean that such practices *are* authoritarian or that they are *perceived* as such. If they are authoritarian, we must work at changing them. If they are not, it is vital that we hang on to the distinction between authority and authoritarianism and explain it to our students. Without it, we are bound to misunderstand the practices.

Bourdieu and Passeron allege that the distinction breaks down in practice because the pedagogical relationship implies the imposition of ideas. Teaching implies imposition. It is true, as we have seen, that the distinction between teacher and pupil implies that one of these has a superior acquaintance with the ideas being studied. The teacher has something to teach, or has been misdescribed, and is entitled to transmit certain ideas. What is transmitted will also reveal what is considered important and significant. These points may all be conceded. There is even a sense in which, if the students are compelled to attend, the ideas are imposed on them. That is, attempts are made to ensure that they encounter certain ideas. It by no means follows, however, that this involves the further attempt to have them accept these ideas. It is this latter attempt which could threaten open-mindedness, if, for example, nonrational methods of persuasion were adopted. But this cannot be inferred from the pedagogical relationship as such. A similar ambiguity bedevils John Holt's discussion of the alleged right to decide what *goes into our minds*.[23] Does the idea enter our minds for consideration or as a belief? If we choose to call it an imposition when we are required to give an idea consideration, this is not an imposition which destroys open-mindedness. Such a judgment would also involve attention to what is being excluded from consideration. That is, the judgment will not be based on the fact of teaching *per se*, but on the way in which the teaching is conducted. Finally, the fact that it is implied that certain ideas are considered important does not itself undermine open-mindedness. This is yet another idea which students can be encouraged to consider to see if they agree. They can be encouraged to reflect critically on this aspect of the hidden curriculum.

Quite possibly Michael Young is right to suggest that we have somewhat hastily concluded that project work and discovery learning in school science have replicated the nature of scientific inquiry. All too often the students are not, and do not see themselves as, theorists in their own right. They are active, of course, by contrast with the passivity of rote learning, but essentially they are following instructions. The problems have been designed by others, deemed important by others, and the methodology determined by others. No doubt this is part of what Friedenberg has in mind when he speaks of the metaphysical absurdity of schooling, since the nature of scientific inquiry is just not like this. Science itself is not presented scientifically in a teaching situation, and thus even in this area open-mindedness is lost.

There is an enormous assumption at work here, however, namely, that the only way to learn X is to practise X in a full-blooded way. But the fact is that school children are *not* yet scientists, and never will be unless they practise various routines and acquire certain skills. In recognizing that they must be progressively introduced to genuine problems, and encouraged to find their own, we need not deny that there is an enormous body of knowledge to be mastered. Students need to become acquainted with the best available theories, and brought to understand that these may well be superseded. Moreover, there is no reason why the appropriate links between science and technology, and between academic and nonacademic science, cannot be made clear. It is not in the interests of open-minded inquiry, however, to allow a political agenda to persuade us to deny that there is any relevant difference between physics and ceramics. And it is the merest ideological nonsense to suggest that a genuine understanding of science cannot be promoted in schools in a capitalist society.

In response to Friedenberg, we must admit that school learning is often not natural in the sense that spontaneous curiosity is natural. Typically, study in school is required by others and involves tasks which would perhaps be unusual in the ordinary context. The learning situation has also been structured by others. But these facts hardly constitute a metaphysical absurdity. First, though we are compelled to attend, we may still learn from the experience. It is just false to say that alienation must result. Second, the special requirements, for example, written instead of oral comments, can be justified in view of the fact that it is a teaching situation, with the consequent need for assessment.[24] Finally, although the experience has been structured, it by no means follows that the experience is distorted. The questions pursued may be presented as possibly useful, rather than as the only possible questions. Good questions do not arise from nowhere. We can be taught to question, and to be critical about the line of questioning being pursued. Of course, the effect of hegemony may be to prevent us from entertaining doubts about the questions we have been encouraged to pursue. But to be aware of hegemony is to be in a position to attempt to resist it. Gramsci himself observed that "the didactic problem is one of mitigating and rendering more fertile the dogmatic approach which must inevitably characterise these first years."[25] That is, we can look for ways of teaching which will undermine the influence of hegemony.

One assumption which, through the workings of hegemony, has been protected from critical examination until very recently is that women should, in general, occupy a subordinate role to men. Alison M. Jaggar has argued that sexist assumptions are bound to be reinforced if courses in women's studies are taught by a man. Let us agree that such a situation might generate practical difficulties, but we must reject the suggestion that the case presents a contradiction. The assumption in question is open to rational objections, and such objections can be grasped, and made, by either sex. That a man happens to be making them does not imply that only a man could make them. If the questions raised about the traditional stereotypes are good, they are good no matter who raises them. We take a dim, and, it might be said, sexist view of the students if we assume that they cannot make the simple distinction between what is contingent and what is necessary. There is no more a contradiction in the situation than there is in the idea of teaching for autonomy or in a lecture on discovery learning. That there is dependence in the teaching context does not mean that we oppose autonomy. The teacher may lecture yet believe that there is much to be said for learning on your own. The instructor is male, but he does not support the traditional hierarchical relationship.

It is further suggested that a male instructor could not present the issues as well as a female because he would not be able to draw upon his own experiences in discussing prejudice. The analogy is drawn with taking a course in art history from someone who has no direct appreciation of painting. But surely the analogy is flawed. The art historian must have studied paintings and the teacher of feminism must have witnessed prejudice. Both must have reflected on these experiences to develop an understanding and appreciation. But to claim that the teacher of feminism must have personally been subjected to the prejudice in question is akin to the claim that the art historian must also be a painter. For a woman to claim that the man's understanding must fall short of a woman's here, is to claim the very sort of insight which is said to be impossible for a man to have. How is the extent of a man's understanding to be known? Of course, the male instructor will not be able to draw on his own experiences, but why must he? Fresh and personal examples can come from the students. The mere fact that the teacher is a man cannot mean that the issues will not be treated in an open-minded way.

It turns out, however, that feminism cannot be taught in an open-minded way by a woman either, if the logic of Jaggar's argument is pursued. She makes the correct point that objectivity in teaching does not demand neutrality, and even condemns indoctrination as the use of irrational techniques of persuasion. But anyone who fails to act as a committed feminist is at once a sexist. The subject, it seems, "requires instructors who (among many other things) know the truth and advocate true theories."[26] On this view, anyone who pauses to query various claims, or who challenges certain feminist arguments, as any open-minded teacher surely would, is simply not teaching the subject at all. He or she is perpetuating the *status quo* and can only be said to be teaching sexism.

The whole line of argument is fallacious. If a sexist is one who thinks that women should, as such, be discriminated against, it is false to say that the label "sexist" applies to all who are not committed feminists. There are many feminist views which go far beyond the principle which the sexist violates, the feminist views considered here being an obvious case in point. Furthermore, it is not at all clear that passionate advocacy is the most effective way to open up the philosophical issues, even if one is a committed feminist. A very fundamental aspect of philosophy is compromised if particular commitments are demanded of instructors. The notion of truth emerging in discussion is lost if teachers must "know the truth" before they are appointed. Teachers are needed who are anxious to go on asking if what they take to be true really is true, and such open-mindedness is not to be dismissed as covert sexism.

That commitment to rational inquiry, which is the hallmark of the open-minded teacher, has been thought by some to be itself a kind of indoctrination. One source of this idea is the recognition that rationality itself cannot be questioned. Kurt Baier has shown, for example, how the question "Should I follow reason?" degenerates into the tautological question "Is doing what is supported by the best reasons doing what is supported by the best reasons?"[27] But the conclusion which is sometimes drawn, that we can only resort to propaganda for reason in the manner of those whose views are contrary to reason, does not follow. The tautology shows that there could not be a good reason to reject reason in general. The degenerate question "Should I follow reason?" is quite different then from the legitimate question "Should I follow this school of thought?", and the significance of this latter question does not show that there is something arbitrary about the rejection of the former. This is not to say, however, that the value of reason must simply be accepted blindly. We may begin as sceptics and come to see that deliberation is worthwhile. Contrary to Suttle, rational persuasion may work if it is seen to pay dividends by those who have doubted its value. It may also be, as Baier shows, that there are times when other strategies must be adopted and deliberation set aside. But the wisdom of this decision is something which must be determined by appeal to reasons.

The other line of thought which encourages the view that teaching cannot be open-minded holds that everything cannot be open to question. Such a state of affairs would mean that there were no standards. The implication is that about certain matters our minds are closed.

But our teaching is based on these axioms or definitions and, therefore, the basis of our claim to be open-minded is suspect. The first point to be made here is that the concept of education does not require that our standards be beyond criticism. These can be regarded as tentative and subject to revision. It is often the case that in attempting to apply a certain standard we begin to see that it is inadequate. In the second place, however, it may be that certain truths *cannot* be questioned. The fundamental laws of logic, for example, cannot be questioned, because any attempt to question them will presuppose them. We shall not succeed in asking a meaningful question unless the terms employed in the question respect the law of identity. The laws of logic cannot be proven because they are presupposed in proof, yet they cannot be seriously challenged. Hence the suggestion of arbitrariness must be abandoned, and with it any suggestion that rational teaching is just another kind of indoctrination. Indeed, the charge of indoctrination only has sense by contrast with the concept of education and rational teaching.

The claim that all education is indoctrination is a redescription which destroys the very distinction these concepts serve to bring out. If it is suggested that such conceptual revision is necessary because the alleged distinction is spurious, then we need to insist that there is an important difference between the case in which a reason is not given when *it is vital* and that in which it is not given because *none could in principle be given*. The latter case can give rise to no sensible protest, but the former is objectionable. We shall not be able to make the relevant objection if the distinction is obliterated, hence we should resist the proposed redescription.

If we are to resist the false idea that teaching is to be contrasted with other, more open-minded strategies like guiding, stimulating, and discovery learning, we must distinguish between fashionable stereotypes of teaching and the logic of the concept. We must distinguish between what comes to mind when we think of teaching and what is logically implied by teaching.[28] Socrates and Descartes wanted to dissociate themselves from the professional context of teaching, with the potentially corrupting influence of financial reward. But this is obviously not to attack the activity of teaching *per se*. Similarly, we may be anxious to criticize an entrenched approach to teaching which is hectoring, authoritarian, and generally miseducative. An alternative may be sketched in terms of discovery learning and facilitation. But it is vital to see that it is an alternative form of teaching which is being recommended, not an alternative to teaching. It is not the teaching of specific moral content which makes for indoctrination, but the way in which that teaching is carried out.

CONCLUSION

The argument has been that there is nothing in the concept of teaching as such, nor in the teacher-student relationship, which rules out the possibility of open-mindedness. There is no reason to believe that ideally the context of schooling or the sex of the teacher need present insuperable problems for the ideal of open-mindedness. The attempt to show that open-minded teaching is a form of indoctrination fails. None of this is to say that teaching is always, or necessarily, open-minded – simply that there is no incompatibility between the two concepts.

When teaching occurs in an institutional context, we may wonder if it is important for those who administer the institution to respect this attitude. This raises the next question to be pursued in this book, the place of open-mindedness in the context of educational administration.

CHAPTER SIX

Open-mindedness in Administration

Is open-mindedness an administrative virtue or liability? So much confusion surrounds the concept of open-mindedness that an intuitive response, if we had one at all, would not be very useful. Let us be clear then that open-mindedness is that attitude which is manifested in our ability and willingness to form and revise views in the light of evidence and argument. Even with this clarification, however, our reactions to the question may be uncertain. Herbert Simon has shown how most administrative principles have an equally plausible but inconsistent running mate.[1] In the context of open-mindedness, we may think at once of the process of consultation and endorse the attitude in question. On the other hand, it will surely be pointed out that decisiveness is an important quality and doubts about the attitude may arise. Certainly it is sometimes maintained that decisiveness and flexibility are mutually exclusive.[2] The issues here are philosophical in character because the problem concerns the logical relationships among certain ideas. The task is to raise the discussion above what Simon called the proverbial level, and the appropriate method is a careful conceptual inquiry. We can begin by examining some general issues which arise if open-mindedness is linked, as I suggested above, with rational inquiry.

RATIONAL DECISION MAKING

Although the two concepts are by no means equivalent,[3] open-mindedness is an aspect of rationality because the attitude involves being disposed to have one's views based on rational considerations. Evidence and argument are all important. But it may be objected that open-mindedness could in fact conflict with rational decision making: "If an administrator, each time he is faced with a decision, must perforce evaluate that decision in terms of the whole range of human values, rationality in administration is impossible."[4] The remark occurs in the context of a discussion of organizational loyalties, and it brings home the point that there is a certain value in having a commitment to the aims of the institution in question. But this value can only be taken as absolute at the cost of ignoring those situations where other values do take precedence.[5] It is beside the point to object that such cases are rare and unusual, since the fact that they are possible is sufficient to create a problem for inflexible loyalty.

Should we then conclude that here is yet another example where an administrative principle conflicts with an equally attractive rival? Simon suggested that problems arise through viewing what are really proverbs or slogans as principles at all, rather than as criteria which are relevant. They need to be considered, but also balanced against each other.[6] There is, however, an obvious difficulty about applying this solution to the principle of open-mindedness itself, for this is the principle which precisely requires that relevant criteria be considered and balanced. The attitude of open-mindedness cannot itself be a negotiable criterion, since it is the principle which is presupposed in our approach to criteria.

The apparent conflict between open-mindedness and loyalty is to be resolved by viewing loyalty as important but not as absolute. Open-mindedness does not conflict with loyalty as such, only with unthinking loyalty. It is the conflict which, in the context of loyalty to one's friends, Socrates pointed to when he advised Crito: "... your zeal is invaluable, if a right one; but if wrong, the greater the zeal the greater the danger; and therefore we need to consider whether I shall or shall not do as you say."[7] Does this mean then that every decision must be made *sub specie aeternitatis*? This, as Simon has shown, would be a prescription for administrative disaster because it would be self-defeating. In trying to arrive at perfect decisions, we would fail even to arrive at adequate ones. What we can do, however, is to remain prepared to modify, or even abandon, our organizational commitment if overriding considerations should arise. It is this stance which captures our open-mindedness, and which is undermined when we think exclusively of administrative skills. Certainly, one can be open-minded about which skills are required to achieve certain goals, but the language of skills leaves the question of aims unexamined.[8]

It will not do, of course, to try to legislate open-mindedness about aims out of the picture, by suggesting perhaps that the very concept of administration concerns the execution rather than the formation of policies. The objection to this is not just that this would be a highly controversial analysis of administration,[9] but that it attempts to derive a normative position from a definition.[10] It is always open to an administrator to judge that he should not administer a particular policy and, in this way, open-mindedness is retained.

The error referred to here is a special case of the general mistake of trying to infer values directly from facts. But the fact/value distinction may generate its own scepticism about open-mindedness, if we are influenced by old-fashioned logical positivism.[11] Impressed by the view that only factual claims can be "correct," we may be tempted to conclude that rational assessment is only possible for means, not for ends. Simon, for example, suggested that "any statement that contains an ethical element, intermediate or final, cannot be described as correct or incorrect, ... the decision-making process must start with some ethical premise that is taken as 'given'."[12] Although echoes of this once dominant view can still be found in textbooks on administration,[13] it would hardly be necessary to deal with the matter here were it not for the fact that it has become fashionable to deny that there is a distinction between fact and value at all.[14] This is equally misguided. That there is a difference between fact and value is clear, since one can say that such and such *is* the case without thereby saying, or implying, that it is *desirable* that such and such is the case. The difference, however, is not that factual judgments admit of rational assessment and evaluative claims do not, but that they are to be assessed in different ways.[15] Value judgments are not simply "given," nor are they arbitrary assumptions. We might, for example, try to show that certain values are presupposed in the very activity of serious questioning or justification.[16] Again, we can ask if we can sincerely assent to a particular value judgment, knowing that, in hypothetical circumstances, it might apply to our own circumstances.[17] Rational discussion of values is surely possible, and thus open-mindedness, which only applies in the context of rational assessment, has application with respect to aims.

It is perhaps also worth noting that open-mindedness about means is not lost when such decisions are classified as factual. Not only is factual error possible (making revision necessary); it is highly likely, given that we must so often decide before we have had an adequate opportunity to determine the facts. If we can correct such errors at subsequent stages of the administrative process, it would be only reasonable to do so. The point here is that "factual" characterizes the *kind* of judgment in question and does not, as it can elsewhere, indicate that the judgment is conclusively verified.

The fallibility of human judgment, the complexity of decision making in organizations, and the emergence of less authoritarian models of management have all contributed to the development which now sees consultation as a central concept in administrative theory. It is useful to recall that it has not always enjoyed the present degree of support. Descartes was confident, for example, that "the great prosperity of Sparta was due, not to the goodness of each of its laws in particular, ... but to their having been devised by a single man, and thus tending to a single end."[18] But this kind of view is now very much out of fashion, and consultation has become part of the proverbial wisdom. Its value, however, is more widely accepted than it is understood. Robin Barrow acutely pointed up the absence of serious work on this concept when he asked "what precisely is meant by notoriously vague phrases such as 'listen to' and 'consult with', when it is argued that the head should listen to and consult with his staff?"[19] Indeed, he might have said "when it is asserted" rather than "when it is argued," for it is argument which is lacking. We shall see, in due course, that Barrow's own comments on this concept are far from being adequate.

THE PROCESS OF CONSULTATION

It is necessary to begin with some fundamental conceptual points, since the literature on administration finds the notion of consultation being used in some curious ways. What, or who, is consulted can be very different from case to case, but what occurs in each case is the same. There are, of course, many different styles and approaches, but this is not to say that there are different concepts of consultation. Persons, books, drawings, – even the stars! – may be consulted, but a common element is found in the fact that a kind of questioning, which may be implicit or explicit, is going on. Someone is trying to learn something, though what is to be learned will vary from case to case.

This fundamental point is neglected by those who are prepared to speak of "information only" consultation.[20] If the management of a company merely transmits information to the work-force periodically, the concept of consultation does not belong here at all. It cannot be suggested that this is a different form of consultation, for this process conflicts with an essential feature of the concept. If, for example, a teacher transmits information to his students, it will not be said that the students have been consulted. Had the students sought the information, we could say that they had consulted their teacher. Consultation is either a one-way process of inquiry, or a two-way (or more) exchange in which the parties both seek and give. The expression "information-only" consultation can only be understood as involving a countermanding adjective.

While all cases of consultation contain the common element identified above, there are in fact two distinct, though often related, purposes in the inquiry process. The difference corresponds to the fact/value distinction and can be roughly captured by the contrast between consultation for information versus advice. We need to remember, however, in drawing the contrast in this way, that we can be advised both what is the case and what we ought to do. The latter divides into advice about means and advice about ends. As we shall see, the ambiguous nature of "advice" and the fact that at one and the same time we can be seeking both information and advice invites confusion and misunderstanding. Let us turn first to consultation for information, including in this category details about what is the case and what is needed to achieve certain stated aims.

It is not surprising that in this context what has been called the "expert-service" model has been influential.[21] The notion of expertise fits well with matters concerning knowledge of what the facts are and how to bring certain things about. It fits less well with questions concerning aims, for the notion of an expert on values is a strange one. When we receive expert advice, for example, this would be advice on how best to achieve certain aims which were not in dispute. We would be more inclined to characterize advice about aims themselves as valuable or helpful rather than expert. The first point to be made then about the model is that it is a limited concept of consultation. Although, as we have seen earlier, rational appraisal of aims is possible, nevertheless we cannot simply be informed what they are by experts. At some point, we have to decide what they are to be.

No doubt the model can be criticized as ineffective and counter-productive in many contexts, but here I want to call attention to two ways in which the notion itself may mislead us. First, the practice of calling in the expert consultant when our own efforts have failed, may lead us to conclude erroneously that the model is restricted to situations where an *existing* problem cannot be resolved. We need to remember that consultation with experts is possible and may be desirable when the objective is to try to uncover hidden or future problems. There is no conceptual problem in being informed about these, and we need to remain open-minded about such matters. Second, in calling in an expert it is not implied that the person inquiring is totally ignorant or uncertain. We often consult diaries, programs, and schedules simply to check or confirm something. Indeed, that which is consulted may not even be regarded as terribly reliable, though the ascription of "expert" implies a degree of confidence. Here we must believe that the source has *something* to contribute. But this does not mean that the model commits us to the closed-minded acceptance of the expert's judgment. We cannot seriously be said to be consulting at all, if we are not prepared to have our beliefs influenced by what we are told. Open-mindedness, however, could not require that we give up our own judgment.

Typically, a rather simplistic view of the link between consultation and open-mindedness appears in the literature on administration, mainly in the context of consultation for advice. The view is that the process of consultation presupposes an open mind in the sense that the person consulting has not made up his or her mind.[22] Now it is a condition of seriously asking for advice that a person accepts the possibility of being guided by whatever advice is given. Clearly, this demands open-mindedness in the sense of being willing to give serious attention to the advice. But this does not mean that the person must be quite undecided when he or she consults. Tentative positions may have been adopted, and the person consulting may even think it quite unlikely that any revision will be called for. All the same, the concept of consultation will evaporate if the person is not willing to make revisions which are warranted. It is easy to see why it is vital to understand what a person is seeking in consulting another. A person may have decided what to do in a given situation and be merely trying to ascertain how others will react to the decision. If this is misunderstood as a request for advice, it is bound to bring the charge of "bad faith."

The importance of clarity here is apparent if we consider the following remarks by Robin Barrow: "Can the head legitimately claim to have listened and consulted with his staff if he subsequently acts contrary to their advice? If not, it seems that these friendly phrases mask a straight-forward demand for entrusting the running of the school to the staff as a whole; if so, it seems that 'consultation' is a procedure without teeth."[23] Attention to the concept of open-mindedness points the way to the solution of this apparent dilemma. First, of course, the head may only have consulted the staff in the sense of trying to learn in advance how they would be likely to react. But let us assume that the head does indeed seek advice. Second, then, we need to insist that one can sincerely seek advice, yet decide not to accept, or act on, that advice. Indeed, if the head were bound to act on the advice, it would not be possible to consider it in an open-minded fashion. But does this mean then that the process imposes no constraints on the administrator, that it is, in Barrow's words, a procedure without teeth? Not at all, but the nature of the constraint needs to be understood. It is a constraint on anyone committed to acting in a reasonable way, just as a moral obligation imposes a constraint on someone who wants to adopt the moral point of view. This is not, of course, the same as a legal restriction, but this is no reason to deny that it is a restriction at all. Consultation implies open-mindedness, and the process therefore has all the constraints which come with a commitment to rationality.

It may, in addition, be deemed necessary to have a formal requirement that consultation occur, and mechanisms in place whereby administrators can be called to account. At the same time, however, it is worth remembering that an individual will normally find it in his or her own interest to consult seriously. Occasions will almost certainly arise when one really needs information and advice from others, and these are not likely to be forthcoming if the process of consultation has been abused in the past. There is a real danger of raising the charge of "bad faith" unfairly if we operate with a confused concept of consultation. For example, it is claimed that "the goal of all consultation is change, whether it be in individuals, groups, organizations, or a community."[24] But while it is true that open-mindedness requires that we be open to the *possibility* of change, it is perfectly conceivable that serious consultation might show that change was not necessary or desirable. We cannot infer that the consultation was not serious from the absence of change. Again, proverbial wisdom can prevent an appreciation of this point.

ON NOT BEING WISHY-WASHY

A major obstacle to a proper understanding of the value of open-minded reflection arises from the "do-something" school of thought.[25] In policy-making sessions, the need to "do something" is expressed when the discussion becomes difficult. It is true, of course, that there will come a point when further discussion is counter-productive. But the fallacy here is that of thinking that while we are talking we are doing nothing, or that of thinking that any decision would be better than none at all. We may rightly suspect at times that the process of "consultation" is an excuse to avoid having to make a decision,[26] but this is an abuse, not a feature, of consultation. If we take "change" as the goal, and operate with a naïve concept of "doing" something, we will find it difficult to make sense of Barnard's excellent point that "the decision may be not to decide. This is a most frequent decision, and from some points of view probably the most important."[27] Unexamined clichés are in danger of destroying this insight.

Conceptual confusion also lies behind the view expressed recently that open-mindedness and decisiveness are not compatible.[28] It is not difficult to piece together the thinking which lies behind this sort of claim. For example, one meaning commonly ascribed to "decisiveness" is promptness in making the decision. Again, if we analyse the notion of decisiveness, we would no doubt speak in terms of the person "who makes up his mind and is not easily moved from his position, capable of making decisions and of standing firm in them."[29] The connotations here of dispatch, independent-mindedness, and resolve may have the cumulative effect of suggesting that open-mindedness and consultation conflict with decisiveness. Open-mindedness may begin to sound like a euphemism for fence-sitting and indecision.

The first point in response is surely that to the extent that being decisive is thought to demand snap judgments, it is hard to see why it should be thought of as a desirable administrative trait at all. It is perfectly obvious that many problems demand long and careful consideration. If, on the other hand, promptness is to be understood as calling for action at the appropriate and opportune moment, then rational reflection is necessary in order to judge when the moment has arrived. If premature decisions are to be avoided, open-mindedness is vital. The administrator who stands firm against pressure to make a hasty decision does not deserve to be called indecisive. Nor is it relevant, in the second place, to point out that in consulting others, he is abandoning independent-mindedness. To be decisive one must be capable of making up one's mind, but this does not require that one eschew advice and counsel. To establish the charge of indecisiveness, one would have to show that indeed the person's mind is made up *for him*. Clearly, this is not a necessary consequence of consultation.

No doubt it is the idea of standing firm, of resolve and determination which is seen as the main threat to open-mindedness. Clearly decisive action could be preceded by open-minded inquiry, but would not such a decision put an end to open-mindedness? Now it must be admitted here that some decisions are, as Simon has brought out, irrevocable in the sense that they bring about a new situation from which there may be no going back.[30] Second, we would lose the notion of decisiveness if the person could be readily moved. But in circumstances where a reconsideration is possible, there is no reason in principle why this must be altogether excluded. There will be a strong presumption against revision, but events may be such that revision would be desirable. One of the factors to be weighed in such a decision would be the effect of revision on our claim to be reliable and decisive.

It is important to notice that in adopting the process of consultation, one is not thereby endorsing a policy of minimal change, what Donna Kerr has called the approach of the "wise slug."[31] This might well merit the charge of indecisiveness in the sense that it could be a recipe for avoiding significant change. But consultation might reveal that dramatic and urgent intervention is called for, and we must not close our minds to this possibility. This is not to say, however, that fence-sitting is always properly regarded as indicating indecision. It is possible to judge that the appropriate position to adopt is one of neutrality, and this decision can be made clearly and unambiguously. This is a decision not to decide in favour of one side to the dispute in question, and may require great courage. The view that, for example, the policy of nonalignment is wishy-washy is a controversial, political judgment. It is not a conceptual truth.

Of course, it is possible to consult others when it is quite unnecessary to do so. But let us be clear that the principle of open-mindedness does not require that we engage in pointless consultation. Unless the situation is such that it is important to go through the exercise of consulting others, it may be immediately clear what needs to be done. Similarly, it may be apparent that further consultation on an issue would be counter-productive. Open-mindedness requires that decisions be formed in the light of evidence and argument, and does not require us to refuse to admit that the evidence is in and the arguments exhausted. Hence open-mindedness is not an invitation to needless delay and indecision. Moreover, consultation does not necessarily seek a middle-of-the-road position, where compromise is the central concept. Sometimes, of course, compromise will be required, but any such proposal is itself something about which we can, and should, remain open-minded.

Indeed, *without* open-mindedness there is a real danger of indecisiveness, as Barnard has shown. It is a fact of administrative life that various codes will come into conflict, and it is vital that the administrator be capable of further reflection designed to resolve the clash. If such ability is absent, we may find "paralysis of action, accompanied by emotional tension, and ending in a sense of frustration, blockade, uncertainty, or in loss of decisiveness and lack of confidence."[32] But what of the concomitant danger of destroying a code altogether if it is overridden by another? It seems to me that, if we are aware of the decision we are making, what should develop is a proper sense of the limitations of the code in question, not a sense of its uselessness. The code comes to be seen as limited and nonabsolute, but nevertheless as relevant.

THE CONTEXT OF EDUCATION

In many institutions and organizations, the aims and objectives are clear and noncontroversial. Open-mindedness is, in practice, restricted to reflection on ways to achieve the stated aims. The situation, however, is quite different in the context of an educational institution because the aims are either expressed in intolerably vague language or are by no means universally endorsed. There is, moreover, the constant danger of being swayed by whatever happens to be fashionable. Consider, for example, the "back-to-basics" movement. We need to ask, first, what exactly this aim would involve, second, does it capture something important in the idea of education, and third, if it is something more than an exaggerated reaction to other views. It is vital, therefore, that those involved in decision-making in the educational context should remain open-minded about the question of aims. It is for this reason that one must beware of thinking of the educational administrator's task exclusively in terms of skills, though skills have their place.

A second consideration in favour of open-mindedness arises to the extent that the educational administrator is expected to show educational leadership. The argument here derives from the fact that open-mindedness is itself a characteristic of the educated person.[33] This condition is clear once we recognize that an educated person has a commitment to truth. No such commitment could be ascribed to a person who was not prepared to form and revise his views in the light of evidence and argument, that is, who was not open-minded. This attitude then is a necessary condition of being educated. It follows then that the administrator who is not open-minded fails to provide a model of an educated individual and in this way is inauthentic.[34] He could not be demonstrating *educational* leadership.

The third reason for stressing the ideal of open-mindedness in education in the contemporary context is simply that many distorted versions of this principle have enjoyed wide circulation, including permissiveness, neutrality, equal time, relativism, and thoroughgoing democratization. Open-mindedness has itself been sloganized, with the result that many who have the responsibility for decision-making in education are operating with a confused idea of open-mindedness. The education of administrators needs to include a critical appraisal of these and other ideas which masquerade as principles of open-mindedness. Too often, that which bears a superficial resemblance to the attitude is uncritically accepted for the attitude itself.

CONCLUSION

The main contention in this chapter is that there is a good deal of confusion about the idea of open-mindedness which leads to it being undervalued, or even rejected, as a principle of administrative behaviour. It is surely necessary to expose the sources of this confusion when even sophisticated theorists like Andrew Halpin can conclude that "to be decisive and to get things done in a world of action, the role of The Operator or of The Planner imposes on them the expectation that they will be dogmatic."[35] Properly understood, open-mindedness does not conflict with other desirable administrative traits such as decisiveness, and is logically bound up with the important process of consultation. Many of the points are implicit in the classic texts, especially in Barnard, but these truths are in danger of being abandoned in casual and oversimplified commentary. This chapter seeks to identify those errors in reasoning which lead to open-mindedness and consultation being dismissed as undesirable or feeble. It suggests that the attitude is especially important in the context of education. An interesting empirical project would be to try to show how *in practice* an administrator could succeed in appearing both open-minded and decisive.

CHAPTER SEVEN

Open-mindedness in Science

Not surprisingly, open-mindedness is one of a number of ideals invoked in attempts to characterize the nature of scientific inquiry. In science, we expect dogmatism, prejudice, and personal preference to be set aside in favour of an open-minded inquiry which strives for objectivity, impartiality, and intellectual honesty.[1] The ideal of objectivity, however, is not to be confused with absolute certainty and infallibility. Scientific theories have a tentative character, subject to revision and outright rejection.[2] Objectivity means rather that independent and public standards must be appealed to in the assessment of scientific claims. Open-mindedness cannot, of course, guarantee that such standards will be satisfied, but it recognizes their supremacy and the vulnerability of scientific theories. This attitude then is part of our notion of the scientific attitude itself, though it is by no means confined to the area of science. It is a vital aspect of any rational inquiry, and for that reason is fundamental to our conception of education. When we think, however, of the dogmatic attitudes which have infected many supposedly rational inquiries, it is not difficult to understand why open-mindedness has commonly been seen as preeminently manifested in science. And in popular stereotypes, open-mindedness and science go hand in hand.[3]

It might be said, however, that the above sketch of the relationship between open-mindedness and science harks back to a myth which has been effectively debunked.[4] The enormously influential work of Thomas Kuhn,[5] in particular, is widely held to have exposed the traditional ideals of science as naive and simple-minded. At times, one has the impression that a nod in the direction of Kuhn ought to suffice to silence any latter-day proponent of the ideal of rationality. This fashionable view, whether or not it reflects an accurate reading of Kuhn, would itself warrant a defence of open-mindedness in the context of science, if that ideal is not to suffer by default. The matter of interpretation is, of course, a vexed one, and it will not be possible in this context to become very deeply involved in the vast enterprise which Kuhnian commentary has become. Certainly, many have held that Kuhn depicts science as closed-minded, and have mounted a powerful attack on that view.[6] Others have suggested, however, that we should not take Kuhn literally when he speaks of "the abandonment of critical discourse" in science.[7] Again, when it is said that Kuhn depicts science in a certain way, are we to understand this to be a description of science or a claim about what is logically possible in science? And with respect to science education, is Kuhn *describing* or *prescribing* indoctrination?[8]

Our primary concern is not with Kuhnian exegesis but with certain philosophical issues surrounding the notion of open-mindedness in science and science education brought to the fore by Kuhn's work. These issues divide into two broad groups. First, there is the question of the very *possibility* of open-mindedness in science. Second, if open-mindedness is not in principle excluded, there is the question of the *desirability* of this attitude both in science and in the teaching of science. Nothing, therefore, hinges on any particular interpretation of Kuhn which may be suggested here. The issues have in large measure been provoked by Kuhn's analysis, but they can be examined in their own right. Although there are conflicting interpretations, it is important to ask what our response should be *if* Kuhn is taken in a certain way. There is no question here of entering into "mock combat."[9]

SCIENCE: NORMAL AND EXTRAORDINARY

Kuhn's account of science, complex as it is in detail, is captured in a small group of interrelated concepts. To understand one is to understand all. What Kuhn calls *normal science* is scientific research based on a truly significant scientific achievement which not only solves certain important problems but generates others to be pursued. Such achievements constitute *paradigms* which guide scientific practice by providing standards and procedures in terms of which the research is conducted. Normal science runs into difficulties or *anomalies* when certain problems continue to resist efforts to resolve them, or when unexpected findings are encountered. Such developments may provoke a *crisis* situation in which a new paradigm is sought. At this point, normal science has been replaced by *extraordinary science*. When a new paradigm is achieved, the process has come full circle.

Is open-mindedness possible in normal science? Kuhn depicts the normal scientist as a puzzle-solver,[10] and it is the ideas associated with this description which have led critics to regard normal science as closed-minded. In a well-known comment, Kuhn's characterization of normal science has been denounced as a "closed society of closed minds."[11] And Kuhn has fostered the view to some extent himself by speaking of "the abandonment of critical discourse."[12] There are further signs of closed-mindedness in normal science, for the paradigm is said to create a more rigid definition of the field, with the result that other views are ignored.[13] In addition, ideas are forced into a *preformed* and *relatively inflexible* box.[14] Many other similar comments could be cited if the purpose were to establish a particular interpretation, but enough has been said to show how the charge of closed-mindedness arises with some plausibility. Let us also leave aside for now a discussion of the implications of Kuhn's views taken as a factual account of the behaviour of scientists.

The first point to be made here is that the activity of normal science does not logically rule out open-mindedness. It makes sense to distinguish between two scientists, both of whom are committed to the paradigm, as more and less open-minded. There will, for example, be alternative ways of applying the paradigm to new areas of interest,[15] and about these open-mindedness is possible. Scientists can also be open-minded or closed-minded about the possibility of finding new ways in which the paradigm can be checked, and can demonstrate this when new checks are proposed.[16] Admittedly, such forms of open-mindedness are constrained by the paradigm but none the less real for that, and they are important if normal science is to be fruitful.[17]

Perhaps these limited forms of open-mindedness are thought to pale into insignificance beside the closed-minded allegiance to the paradigm itself. But why is open-mindedness impossible even here? If one is aware that anomalies can occur, it would seem to be possible to be open-minded about claims, or indications, that they have arisen. One reason for rejecting this suggestion is the mistaken belief that this would mean continually calling the paradigm into question.[18] And how can doubt and commitment coexist? The answer to this, however, is that doubt is not required, simply a willingness to call the paradigm into question in certain circumstances. It would be easy to define "paradigm" in such a way that only a dogmatic allegiance would constitute acceptance of the paradigm, but this would be an uninteresting stipulative definition.[19] The important logical point is that there is no incompatibility between being, on the one hand, guided by an unprecedented scientific achievement yet, on the other hand, willing to consider the significance of whatever anomalies happen to arise. This willingness is a form of open-mindedness which can be present during the stage of normal science. It does not imply that paradigm review is under way.

It is when the anomalies become serious that we encounter what Kuhn calls a crisis which may bring about extraordinary science. Kuhn describes the behaviour of scientists during this period in such a way that the concept of open-mindedness cannot apply. Of course, scientists can, and sometimes do, change their views at this stage, and come to accept a new paradigm. We may be tempted at first to view these as open-minded by contrast with their fellow-workers who go to their graves clinging to the old paradigm.[20] But change is not, as such, necessary or sufficient for open-mindedness, and Kuhn's characterization of the change as a "gestalt switch"[21] robs the process of a rational foundation. This latter is crucial since open-mindedness involves forming and revising views in the light of *evidence* and *argument*.

To allow the concept of open-mindedness to have application during the period of extraordinary science, it is necessary to reject the idea that the competing paradigms are incommensurable, that there is no common independent standard to which appeal can be made in resolving conflicts between paradigms. Proponents of different paradigms are said to work in different worlds,[22] and the competition between them cannot be resolved by proofs.[23] What is required is conversion.[24] We may grant at once that such an account often captures the psychology of those involved in the "debate," but it is a separate matter (Kuhn's doubts about the distinction in question notwithstanding)[25] whether or not rational appraisal is in principle impossible. Obviously, no number of actual historical examples of conversion could show that *only* conversion is possible. Even if the new paradigm always were just adopted, or invented, in a relatively sudden gestalt switch, open-minded scientists could set about testing its ability to avoid serious anomalies. The distinction between the context of discovery and the context of justification would remain.[26]

As many other commentators have pointed out,[27] it is trivially true that normal science cannot rationally appraise the merits of competing paradigms, but this is far from showing that rational appraisal itself is impossible. If the paradigms are in any serious sense rivals, there must be some common ground which they share. Without some agreement, there can be no disagreement.[28] If the rival proponents are able to share a paradigm-neutral description of what is observed and predicted behaviour, there is a basis for a common standard. Of course, this description will not be theory-free in any absolute sense, but it could be neutral relative to the theories of the competing paradigms. Before we abandon the idea of paradigms being rationally judged, we need some reason why a neutral way of describing what is seen could not be given. We can readily point to particular cases where relatively neutral descriptions can be found, for example, the fact that the metal screen in Röntgen's laboratory did give a faint glow.[29] It is not possible to show *a priori* that such a description is always available, but similarly there can be no *a priori* argument to the effect that such is logically impossible.

The descriptions in question are only relatively neutral because observation is itself theory-laden.[30] Apparently simple tasks, such as counting the number of people present in a given context, may be bedeviled by underlying theoretical disputes about the concept of person.[31] At times, this is a controversial concept and one's interpretation will affect the results obtained. First, however, the controversial aspects are not *always* present in inquiries which employ this concept. We do not normally have to determine the status of a foetus in order to answer the question how many persons attended a lecture. Second, there is no reason why we cannot continue to discuss the controversial aspects of the concept and hope to arrive at a resolution. Of course, the discussion will have to be conducted in language which is also theory-laden, but it does not follow that these theories must escape critical examination.[32] Although theory is present in observation, such theories are often not in dispute at all. Where they are in dispute, they can be examined. If the relevant concepts are vague or ambiguous, we can aim at greater precision so that accurate observation can proceed. We may need a working definition to distinguish between bottles and jars,[33] but what would it mean (sceptical doubts about illusions, and problems with borderline cases, apart) to wonder if this is really a bottle at all? Unless some such empty worry is involved, it is not clear why we are supposed to conclude that theory-ladenness prevents us "from ever reaching the foundations of sure, objective knowledge."[34]

It is sometimes argued that comparison between paradigms is impossible because paradigms set their own standards and become self-justifying. Any attempted appeal to second-order standards in a paradigm debate will be vitiated by the reappearance of paradigm differences. Criteria of evaluation are, in effect, paradigm-bound. If true, this would certainly make something like the notion of conversion attractive, and open-minded consideration would be lost. We have noted earlier that the paradigm does include standards or criteria which indicate what is a legitimate problem or solution. But this does not mean that the paradigm sets the standards in terms of which the paradigm itself is to be judged. Nor does it show that there cannot be independent standards, shared by competing paradigms, which can be appealed to in resolving paradigm debate. The whole argument, as

Scheffler has shown, confuses internal and external criteria of evaluation.[35] Thus, although in learning a paradigm a scientist acquires an inextricable mixture of theory, methods, and standards, there remains the likelihood of anomalies arising which defy the accepted standards. It can become necessary to ask if there are other standards which lie outside the paradigm.

Open-mindedness has a foothold in the area of extraordinary science only if at some stage competing paradigms can be compared and judged. If this is excluded, as it would be given strong relativism, open-mindedness would degenerate into something like a willingness to change with the times. Those who set the new trend would not be open-minded either, but simply overtaken by an intuitive shift in outlook which cannot, even subsequently, be defended. Often, of course, the emerging paradigm cannot be shown to be more adequate than its older rival in the early stages when a few scientists begin to work with it. Still, there is a sense in which their decision *can* represent open-mindedness, even though a satisfactory defence of the paradigm is absent. A useful distinction here is that between accepting and pursuing a theory.[36] A scientist may decide to work with a theory because it looks promising, interesting, or novel, and this willingness suggests an open-minded outlook in which one is prepared to see where an idea might lead. At some point, however, the notion of evaluation must have application. To be willing to follow up an idea in this way does not mean that one has blindly accepted it.

THE IDEAL OF OPEN-MINDEDNESS IN SCIENCE

If the notion of incommensurability is given up, and open-mindedness becomes possible in principle, it makes sense to ask how important it is as an ideal in science. Here the historical side of Kuhn's work, and the evidence produced by other writers, becomes relevant. The practice of scientists often seems to fall far short of the ideal described earlier in the stereotype. First, Kuhn claims, scientists do not in fact treat anomalies as counter-instances which falsify, or cast doubt on, the paradigm.[37] They devise *ad hoc* modifications to the theory in order to protect the paradigm. Second, as Bernard Barber reports, many innovative scientists have simply found their work ignored by the dominant scientific community.[38] Third, there is the disquieting fact of fraud in science, where researchers have distorted or invented data in order to support their ideas rather than pursuing the truth in a disinterested manner.[39]

It is certainly important to notice that it is not simply opposition from theology and ideology which has stood in the way of open-mindedness in science. The practice of science itself has offended against that ideal. At the same time, we must be careful not to make too much of these findings. First, we only know that frauds have been perpetrated because open-minded inquiry has eventually succeeded in exposing them. Second, the well-known cases are scandalous because they constitute such striking exceptions to the norm. Finally, any attempt to ascribe bias and prejudice in blanket fashion is self-defeating, since such ascriptions themselves rest on research to which the same objections can be made.[40]

Having said this, however, it must be admitted that preconceived ideas often influence our interpretations and can distort our perceptions. In a well-known experiment, subjects were often unable to pick out an anomalous playing card such as a black four of hearts.[41] Our expectations influence our perceptions and can prevent us from noticing a problem or anomaly. In such cases, even if individuals are prepared to take counter-instances into consideration, the necessary conditions for doing so are not met. Thus the individuals in question are not *able* to act in an open-minded manner. As Barber puts it, "scientists sometimes miss discoveries that are literally right before their eyes."[42] In describing this as "resistance," as Barber does, we need to be clear that it does not imply, as it can elsewhere, that the scientist is unwilling to entertain new ideas. It is used rather in that passive sense of an impediment created by one's expectations. The point is important because if scientists *are* willing to look for problems and anomalies, there is no reason to believe that they *must* continue to fail to find them. It will make sense to try to become aware of the biases at work. If we ignore this ambiguity in the notion of resistance, we are more likely to draw pessimistic conclusions about the possibility of open-mindedness in scientific practice.[43]

Just as change can too easily be taken as a sufficient indicator of open-mindedness, so too resistance can be falsely equated with closed-mindedness. It is surely clear, however, that many ideas need to be resisted because they are entirely spurious.[44] But if we keep the concept of open-mindedness firmly anchored to evidence and argument, as indicated above, there is no reason why open-mindedness in science would mean opening the flood-gates to nonsense. Open-mindedness is exercised critically, and will itself demand that certain ideas be resisted. Of course, it has happened that brilliant suggestions have been dismissed as nonsense when first propounded,[45] but these errors have come to light as a result of open-minded reflection. The argument from fads and fallacies, however, provides no justification for ignoring ideas, for we can only be in a position to claim that a theory is nonsensical if it has been critically examined. On the other hand, it is important that scientists not be "lightly distracted" from their work,[46] and sometimes it is an appropriate commitment to a project, rather than closed-mindedness, which leads a scientist to ignore a piece of work.

Kuhn does not help us to appreciate how commitment itself can be open-minded,[47] for at times he has used the notion of *dogma* to characterize scientific commitment.[48] Clearly, however, dogmatism and open-mindedness *are* conceptually at odds. Pointing to the familiar facts of resistance, Kuhn comments that these "do not seem to bespeak an enterprise whose practitioners are notably open-minded."[49] We may agree at once with Kuhn that the individual scientist is very often not open-minded, but it is important not to read closed-mindedness into every case of resistance. Moreover, the concept of dogma hardly applies in the case of a scientist who works with the best corroborated theory of the time. Toulmin is surely right to insist that "it was wholly reasonable – and undogmatic – for physicists between 1700 and 1880 to accept Newton's dynamics as their provisional starting point."[50] If we confuse commitment and closed-mindedness, it will be very difficult to uphold the ideal of open-mindedness in science.

The fact is that there *is* a case to be made for "strongly held convictions" and "deep commitment to a particular way of viewing the world," to use some of Kuhn's own phrases, but this is in no way to endorse dogmatism or closed-mindedness in science. Kuhn, for example, points out that problems are often recognized, and solved, because there is a commitment to the paradigm.[51] *Ad hoc* modifications to the theory in the face of apparent anomalies also indicate a deep commitment which may prove useful in preserving a large part of the original theory. The point which needs to be made here, however, is not that closed-mindedness may on occasion have valuable consequences (though this may be true), but rather that a tenacious defence of a theory is not in itself an instance of closed-mindedness. This is by no means a trivial, terminological dispute. It is an important logical point that one's defence of a theory can be conducted in a critical manner which makes the charge of dogmatism false.

There is no evidence to suggest that open-minded "normal scientists" would be less efficient and capable puzzle-solvers than the dogmatic and uncritical worker characterized by Kuhn.[52] One might be tempted to think that evidence is hardly required here, since the open-minded scientist would be distracted and diverted, chasing down every false but attractive idea which emerged. We have seen, however, that this view rests on a confused notion of open-mindedness which Dewey very clearly exposed.[53] A further point is that the open-minded scientist is surely in a better position to recognize those anomalies which eventually produce a crisis for the paradigm.[54] Kuhn may be correct in claiming that "close eighteenth and nineteenth-century attention either to the work of Ptolemy or the relativistic views of Descartes, Huygens, and Leibniz would have delayed rather than accelerated the revolution in physics with which the twentieth century began."[55] But the discarded theories began to have new relevance in the light of unsolved problems, and open-mindedness is important if these are to be recognized as significant. Kuhn's dogmatic and uncritical scientist is not the sort of person who has a "willingness to let experiences accumulate and sink in and ripen."[56] It is certainly true that one great advantage of normal science is knowing what sorts of results one should obtain, and, as a result, being in a good position to tell when research has gone astray.[57] But this advantage does not depend upon having a dogmatic commitment. Indeed, the latter increases the likelihood that the existence of the problem will be denied or ignored.

Judgment, of course, is indispensable, as Polanyi makes clear.[58] There are no rules for determining when observed deviations from accepted assumptions are significant and when they need to be explained away. Scientists, therefore, must live with an ambiguous attitude towards authority in science: "We have to face then both rejections of authority that are futile and other rejections of authority to which science owes its greatest advances."[59] This dilemma cannot be resolved, however, by creating a central authority in science which might even impose conclusions.[60] Polanyi points out that such authority would destroy science. Conclusions, which are imperfect and provisional, are the result of discussion in the community of scientists. It is here that we find the value of open-mindedness, what Polanyi sometimes calls the principle of tolerance.[61]

Kuhn fails to find open-mindedness and comes to value closed-mindedness through conceptual confusion. He maintains that a scientist requires a commitment to what is "local, arbitrary and temporary." He draws the conclusion that "that portion of the commitment is a closing of the mind, one that inhibits, at the same time that it permits, original research."[62] This assessment, however, blurs the important distinction between those scientists who do, and those who do not, continue to entertain objections to those local, arbitrary, and temporary commitments which they have made. The result of this confusion is the mistaken view that open-mindedness would stand in the way of original research.

SCIENCE EDUCATION

The stereotype of science described in the opening paragraph often appears in comments on science education. Woods and Barrow, for example, claim that "the very nature of scientific activity runs counter to the possibility of indoctrination being practised in science."[63] This view, as we have seen, rests on a controversial account of scientific practice, albeit one which the argument of this chapter has tried to support. In the light of the contemporary debate inspired by Kuhn, however, it is quite inadequate, and even misleading, to make the claim without explanatory comment.

Kuhn himself has denied that he wished to defend the methods of scientific instruction generally employed around 1960,[64] the approach, we can take it, condemned by Schwab in *The Teaching of Science as Enquiry*.[65] Kuhn claimed to welcome the reform movement then under way in science teaching in schools and universities, though he doubted that the reforms could in fact be as successful as proponents hoped they might: "In particular, I wonder to what extent the facts (whether 'authoritative' or not) can be dispensed with in favour of 'methods of investigation'. I suspect that students will learn both together as samples of accepted achievement, which is only to say that I suspect they will learn paradigms."[66] It was noted in the introductory section that there is some dispute whether Kuhn is describing or prescribing indoctrination in science instruction, and comments such as the one just quoted do not yield an unequivocal answer. Kuhnian interpretation aside, however, there are certain important comments about science education which need to be made in the context of open-mindedness.

First, if we take the distinction between facts and methods of inquiry to parallel that between dogmatic and open-minded science instruction, the importance of facts will make it impossible to defend an open-minded approach. We can agree with Schwab in his condemnation of science teaching which amounts to "a nearly unmitigated *rhetoric of conclusions*."[67] To teach a body of *authoritative* facts, however, is not at all the same as to impose a dogma in *authoritarian* fashion. In short, we need not worry if students "learn paradigms," but we must strenuously object if they are being encouraged to hold them in certain ways.

Second, if we think of scientific practice as mainly dogmatic and uncritical, with the exception of extraordinary science, then indoctrination will seem to be a natural and appropriate pedagogical method. Of course, there will remain independent, moral objections to such a practice in that it fails to respect the student's autonomy and independent judgment. But the value of science might well be thought to override such objections, and indoctrination might be justified as a necessary evil. From a practical point of view, therefore, it is important for science education that the objections to the characterization of scientific practice as dogmatic be made clear.

Third, if it is true, as has been claimed,[68] that the rapid growth of science means that paradigms hold sway for shorter periods, then it is increasingly important that scientists be prepared in their training for paradigm review. The closed-minded individual can only be handicapped in the period of extraordinary science. In this connection, quite apart from considerations of honesty, it would seem to be vital that an accurate, undistorted view of the history of science be presented.[69] Alternative, even discarded, views need to be studied if present beliefs are not to generate into dogma.[70] Students of science need to be familiar with the facts of resistance if they are ever to be in a position to try to overcome this tendency. The history and philosophy of science can have an important role to play in fostering an open-minded outlook.

Fourth, if open-mindedness is to be appreciated as a central ideal in science education, it must not be misunderstood through casual association with other notions such as suspended judgment, lack of emotion, scepticism, or tolerance. It is not that these are reprehensible and open-mindedness an absolute value, but simply that they are different. Consequently, objections to these other ideas are not in themselves objections to open-mindedness. What, for example, the Educational Policies Commission discusses under the heading "Questioning of All Things" is precisely the attitude of open-mindedness, though this term as such is not employed.[71] We should not allow the logical and practical difficulties in the idea of questioning all things to undermine the value of open-mindedness.

CONCLUSION

The argument of this chapter has been that the traditional association of science and open-mindedness has not been discredited. We are clearer than before about the many ways in which science can fail to be open-minded, but there is no reason to think that open-mindedness in science is a myth. Given that it is possible in principle, it makes sense to look for ways in which we can work at making it more likely in practice. The value of the attitude in science and in science education can be appreciated if we retain a clear concept of open-mindedness and avoid confusion with other concepts.

CHAPTER EIGHT

Open-mindedness, Liberalism, and Truth

The attitude of closed-mindedness obviously does not preclude the possibility of the closed-minded person having, and coming to acquire, true beliefs. We may cling at all costs to our beliefs and yet those beliefs may be true. Again, we may accept uncritically the teachings of a church or a party, but in so doing come to acquire true beliefs. The attitude specifies the way in which we hold our views, or come to learn them, and does not determine the truth value of those views. Conversely, the open-minded person, who is prepared to form and revise his views as impartially and as objectively as possible in the light of available evidence and argument, may in fact form opinions which are false, may give up opinions which happen to be true, or continue to hold beliefs which ought to be abandoned. Descartes thought that a person always has enough intelligence to understand the conclusions which follow from clear principles by evident reasoning,[1] but it is undeniably the case that when we try to arrive at true conclusions, we often go astray.

We cannot, therefore, claim that closed-mindedness and truth are incompatible, nor that open-mindedness entails truth. And yet a conceptual connection of a different kind can be drawn here. If a person sincerely wants to arrive at true beliefs, or to ensure that his present beliefs are true, then he must recognize a presumption in favour of open-mindedness. If he is not willing to adopt the practice of listening, as Mill put it, "to all that could be said against him,"[2] he is ignoring criticisms and objections which might either show that a certain belief is false, or bring into sharper focus the truth it contains. And, then, where is his concern for truth? The attitude of open-mindedness commits one to examining rival views, and this, in turn, entails a willingness to allow alternative views to be expressed. There can be no guarantee that truth will emerge, nor, contrary to the claims of some, that at least our understanding of the issues will necessarily be improved.[3] Discussions which are entered into with open-mindedness on all sides may, nevertheless, prove to be quite inconclusive and confusing. Furthermore, the presumption in favour of open-mindedness can be defeated. We may, for example, have evidence that an individual or group will seize the occasion to indoctrinate us, and we are not obliged to put our open-mindedness into jeopardy. But these points are quite compatible with the claim that there is a presumption in favour of open-mindedness.

In view of this, it is important that liberal educators look carefully at certain theories and practices which may threaten this ideal. For example, in recent years many educators have vigorously supported the exclusion of certain ideas from school textbooks, and others have wanted certain books banned entirely. These actions have been recommended in the name of open-mindedness, despite the fact that forbidding or controlling access to ideas would seem *prima facie* to run counter to that attitude. On the other hand, the difficulties involved in defining legitimate teacher intervention, whether in classroom talk or curriculum planning, have spawned a plethora of notions which purport to satisfy the demands of open-mindedness while avoiding the problems in question. The adequacy of such notions must be assessed. Let us turn first to the matter of textbook control.

SENSE AND CENSORSHIP

The spectre of censorship is never far away in the context of formal education, because schools are limited access forums such that "any school's curriculum and textbooks reflect decisions that some ideas are to be excluded from the curriculum."[4] We need, however, to consider initially the suggestion that the concept of censorship may not apply *at all* in the context of schooling because "liberal ideas of free expression and censorship apply paradigmatically to laissez faire intellectual markets; that is instances where there is little difficulty involved in getting any idea a hearing."[5] It can, of course, be admitted that traditional liberal views about the need to protect free expression from sanctions need to be supplemented by theories which provide criteria for granting access to forums of communication. The sense in which traditional liberal views do not apply, is that they are not adequate to *govern* cases involving limited access forums. But to grant this, is not to admit that the concept of censorship is not applicable in such forums at all, in the sense that decisions there cannot be counted as cases of censorship, or, at best, are atypical. Movies and the theatre are also limited access forums, but there is no doubt that the notion of censorship fits such contexts.

Thus, if the concept is not, in principle, ruled out, we can ask if the actions of curriculum planners and/or protest groups can be regarded as cases of censorship. We do not normally think of curriculum planning as possibly involving censorship, but are no doubt more inclined to regard the actions of at least some protest groups in this way. But, the point is made, the difference between making and protesting a decision is not "especially interesting."[6] Indeed, "individuals and groups who protest something that is or is not being taught can be conceived not as engaging in attempts at censorship, but merely as attempting to gain influence over the decisions concerning who or what gains access to the forum of the school."[7] Curriculum planners also attempt to influence such access decisions, and therefore if one group is to be charged with censorship, the other group comes in for the same criticism. It might be urged against this alleged parallel that "it makes some difference, for example, whether access decisions are made on grounds of time constraints and comparative value of different activities or whether they are made in order to exclude ideas regarded as noxious."[8] This is indeed a crucial point, but it is resisted on the grounds that "it continues to be the case that in any limited access ideological market decisions which will restrict the availability of ideas (on grounds of comparative worth!) are inevitable."[9]

Certainly, curriculum planners and protest groups are both motivated to some extent by considerations of value, and both argue for decisions which have the effect of restricting the availability of ideas. But it can be shown, I think, that the concept of censorship cannot be applied simply on the basis of the effect of one's actions. This point is blurred in the ambiguous statement that "some ideas are to be excluded." There are clear cases surely where the actual effect of excluding something from a limited access market would *not* count as censorship. The distinction between the critic and the censor does not disappear just because the theatre critic, for example, may be instrumental in terminating the run of a certain play. Furthermore, reference to *mere* influence glosses over the difference between recommending a book for careful study, which may mean in fact that some other book is neglected, and trying to ensure that students are prevented from having any access to certain books or ideas. Detailed case studies have shown that at times the intent has simply been to have certain books or ideas banned by the authorities.[10] This is indeed an attempt to influence, but it is disingenuous to describe it as *mere* influence.

The purpose of the analogy with the critic is simply to show that we cannot ignore the intention and concentrate exclusively on the effect. The school authorities, of course, have the power to legislate their views, but it is still important to ask what their intentions are. It is tempting to seek a way of side-stepping this because it is not at all easy to determine what a person's real intentions are. Censorship can be disguised as curriculum planning. But although there are many difficulties in practice, the conceptual point is that it is one thing to want X *included* (with the result that Y is neglected or ignored), and quite another to want Y *banned*.

The fact, however, that certain ideas will be excluded even though there is no deliberate act of suppression does create some obligation for open-minded teachers to be fairly active in looking for weaknesses in the views they are presenting. They will need also to be aware of the possibility that important books may be neglected. It will be important to try to ensure that legitimate criticisms are not being ignored simply because they have no ready access. Normally, we are prepared to allow that an individual is open-minded if he is willing to consider criticisms which he encounters. We do not insist on an active search for difficulties in the ordinary context. But the situation of limited access, and the fact that an educational institution has a special concern with truth, combine to make the requirements of open-mindedness somewhat more demanding.

We have seen then that the concept of censorship applies even though the school is a limited access forum, and that a distinction can be drawn between curriculum planning and censorship. The distinctive feature of the latter relates to the intention of those in authority to ensure that access to ideas, or the expression of ideas, is forbidden or limited. The concept would then seem to apply to the widespread practice of removing offensive views from textbooks. Favourite targets in recent years have been the various kinds of stereotyping of minority groups which have been found in abundance in school texts. How is one to justify such actions, for justification seems to be called for? Mill gave the dramatic case of the lone dissenter: "... mankind would be no more justified in silencing that one person, than he, if he had the power, would be justified in silencing mankind."[11]

We may perhaps begin by recalling that we are speaking of an educational context, and the concept of education is linked with the concept of truth in the sense that the process of education aims at the promotion of true beliefs. Moreover, the concept of open-mindedness is similarly bound up with that of truth, for the open-minded person is one who tries to be as impartial and as objective as possible in forming or revising his views. The chief virtue of open-mindedness is that it makes possible the assessment of claims to knowledge. Stereotyping, biased presentations, racial prejudice, and falsehood stand in clear opposition to the aims of open-mindedness. Why then should such distortions not be eliminated from textbooks?

The trouble with this argument is that it focuses on the aim and neglects the process of open-minded inquiry. It is an essential feature of the process that truth is to emerge in the course of an inquiry which allows all points of view to be expressed. We may, of course, want to identify a view as distorted, and open-mindedness does not preclude taking a stand on this. But this is not yet to justify suppression. Suppose, however, that we take note of the fact that "textbooks reflect a social commitment to certain mandatory curriculum content."[12] The students are required to use certain texts, and come to regard these as authoritative. It is, therefore, surely important to ensure that the texts are as accurate as possible, and this may mean that certain views will have to be suppressed.

There are at least two obvious objections to this line of thought. First, we again move too quickly in speaking of suppression, because a view which is presented in a text may equally be countered in the same text. Whether or not open-mindedness is satisfied here will very much depend upon the way in which the rejected view is presented. If the weaknesses of a position are to be indicated, there is an obligation to bring out the strengths in the position also.[13] We can hardly be serious about the problem of distortion if we ourselves present distorted accounts of the opposition. Second, it may properly be pointed out that the attitude in question of regarding the text as authoritative presents a problem. Students should surely be encouraged to develop a healthy critical attitude towards the texts they are using. The practical difficulties involved in eliminating bias and prejudice mean that students must be encouraged to look for these in their reading. It must not be implied that the attitudes in the text are beyond question, for we become aware of subtle forms of prejudice which we had once neglected.

An example of this is the prejudice which can be implicit in examples and illustrations accompanying subject matter which is not concerned in itself with the attitudes conveyed in this way. In this sort of case "because the representation ... is not the explicit subject matter of most of the textbooks in schools, students almost never have the opportunity to discuss the accuracy of that representation; these portraits of various groups are simply unexamined impressions left with the student."[14] The author has in mind an arithmetic text which portrays blacks in a distorted way. He makes the point that we shall not be teaching arithmetic at all if the lesson is taken up with a discussion of the accuracy of the impression. Similarly, we might add, a discussion in the text itself will take us away from the subject matter also. These points, incidentally, do not imply that subjects need to be studied in isolation from each other. And it may be argued that the impression could be examined in some other appropriate lesson.

This, of course, is a possibility. And teachers ought to feel free to criticize aspects of texts being used by their colleagues, if the school is serious about promoting a healthy atmosphere of criticism. Nevertheless, if such impressions are removed from the arithmetic text, surely the criterion of relevancy can be invoked to justify this. We cannot be accused of suppressing an alternative point of view because the attitude towards blacks conveyed in the representation is not a point of view *on the subject in question* at all. To remove this impression is not to engage in any kind of censorship; it is, rather, to attempt to stick to the subject at hand. We do not need to defend this sort of exclusion in terms of "a more complex ethics of communication."[15] It is enough that the representation is gratuitous. If accompanying examples and illustrations are bound to create *some* impression, then, in the absence of an opportunity to discuss such impressions, it is important that the impressions be as accurate as possible. Open-mindedness aims at the truth, and this aim is frustrated by distorted impressions which must in the context remain unexamined. The criterion of relevancy is, of course, open to abuse, and people may appeal to it in order to suppress points of view which really are relevant but which they would prefer to have excluded. But this does not show that the criterion is inappropriate in the sort of case discussed above, only that any appeal to it must be carefully examined.

Clearly, this sort of argument is not applicable when the attitudes conveyed do relate to the subject matter of the text. But here, a limited kind of exclusion can be defended on other grounds. No one will object if a teacher sets out to avoid bias and prejudice in his own talk and behaviour. Indeed, open-mindedness *requires* that a teacher aim at this. But then, in so far as the textbook is viewed as an extension of the teaching performance, the same aim is required. The teacher, therefore, is entitled to try to ensure that the text is not itself prejudiced, that it is accurate and fair-minded. This will mean, however, that existing prejudices must be reported and described as accurately as possible. There is no justification in this argument for suppressing such a procedure.

It might be urged at this point that facts which might present certain groups in an unfavourable light, and thus encourage prejudice, ought to be suppressed. And certainly, a sensitive teacher will often judge it desirable to avoid certain topics in certain circumstances. Nevertheless, there is a strong presumption in favour of truth, and this is part of the very notion of serious inquiry. To pretend that certain things did not happen is not to be writing history, but rewriting it. To overturn the presumption, we would need very good evidence that learning the truth in that context would frustrate educational goals. And in making any decision, we would have to consider the consequences of suppressing the facts for our own commitment to the pursuit of truth, and for our students should they subsequently discover the deception. And almost certainly they will.

SLOGANS FOR STRATEGIES

The difficulties involved in drawing a line between legitimate restriction and objectionable censorship in education has surely contributed to the popularity of many proposed ways of by-passing the problem. Some liberals have frankly despaired of reconciling the idea of teacher influence with the demands of open-mindedness. The felt dilemma is captured in the following question where the contradiction is thought to be self-evident: "How does a teacher 'ask if honesty is more important than kindness in a particular situation' while at the same time declaring his own answer, and at the same time encourage inquiry?"[16] But it is only when we are bewitched by conceptual confusion that this question seems baffling. We prevent ourselves from recognizing the perfectly ordinary case of an answer being given *in a certain sort of way*, that is, an answer which communicates one's interest in the reactions of the students, and one's willingness to reconsider the answer in the light of such reactions.

One source of the confusion here is located in those considerations which account for the persistent appeal of the doctrine of neutrality. Many educators hold that teacher neutrality is logically required in education. Consider, for example, the following view: "Of course, the teacher has his own views on history, science, literature, politics and everything else: but he is not there to sell them – he is there to help his pupils form their own views reasonably."[17] It must, of course, be admitted that a certain kind of non-neutrality, the blind championing of a particular point of view, does threaten educational values including open-mindedness. But it is simply a mistake to regard "selling one's views" as the necessary consequence of non-neutrality.[18] Pejorative labels such as "selling" and "proselytizing" do not encourage us to consider other forms which non-neutrality might take. Instead of traditional, dogmatic moralizing, it might take the form of an open-minded defence of a particular point of view. We need to remember that "It is language which expresses possibilities of meaning, possibilities of what can and cannot be said. So a decline in the language ... represents a decline in what can be said."[19] To fall in with the sort of language used above is to begin to lose sight of the fact that the attitude of open-mindedness can be adopted towards beliefs *which we hold* inasmuch as we remain willing to revise or reconsider them. This is, for example, the attitude which Socrates is urging on Meno when he says that their conclusions must not merely have seemed right when they arrived at them, but continue to seem right now and in the future.[20] He could not have been urging Meno to remain neutral, since Meno was not by this point neutral; and he was not urging him to become neutral, but only to adopt those views which can be defended.

We may, however, encounter the view that open-mindedness *demands* neutrality, at least in one sense of open-mindedness. Here appeal will be made to the case in which a person is, as we say, "keeping an open mind," where this means that the person has not made up his mind. This case is distinguished from that in which a person is said to be open-minded about some of his views. But though there are differences here, we need to resist the fashionable tendency to postulate several senses. What we find here are not different senses but different contexts. The same attitude or willingness is present in each of these cases, though in one it is adopted in the process of forming a view whereas in the other it comes into the process of reconsidering a view previously adopted. In a similar way, we do not have two senses of teaching when we are teaching for an enriched understanding as opposed to an initial understanding. The difference lies in the context. Thus, while the open-minded person is sometimes neutral, there is no necessary link here and no reason why the open-minded teacher must seek to avoid influencing the student towards a particular point of view.

A similar confusion relates to a certain connotation of the term "open-mindedness," and this has been seized on by Douglas Stewart in a comment on my own earlier work: "There are other educationally relevant uses of open-mindedness which pick out dispositions of mind not included in Hare's analysis. For example, the parent or teacher who grants a great deal of latitude to children with respect to their behaviour is said to be open-minded. This use of the term implies the disposition to be permissive. It is this sense of 'open-mindedness' which has been to the fore in debates between traditional and progressive educators."[21] I do not wish to deny that people may at times use the term "open-mindedness" to capture what is meant by that excessively vague term "permissive." It is vital, however, to be clear that when this happens, they are referring to a disposition which is not logically related to the original concept at all. This can readily be shown. A person who is quite closed-minded may not care what others believe and as a result may be quite permissive. Again, a teacher may be permissive, but merely go along mindlessly with fashionable trends. Such a teacher may be empty-headed but not open-minded.

We need not regard it as a decisive objection that ordinary language countenances the link which is disputed here. As we have seen above, ordinary talk can begin to obliterate certain distinctions. It can be shown, as I have just indicated, that the logic of the concepts is not the same. Moreover, it is not difficult to see how one can slide from one meaning to the other. For example, the forms which these distinct traits take are often remarkably similar. It is important to head off this slide if we can, for a reason which R.M. Hare brings out in a comment on permissiveness when he observes that the choice facing us is not between prohibiting things and permitting them.[22] The central question concerns what *ought* to be permitted and prohibited. There is a presumption in favour of open-mindedness, though there will be occasions when it will be better not to be open-minded. But we are neutral about permissiveness until we know what is being permitted. If we equate the two, open-mindedness can lose its status as an educational ideal by association with a quite different disposition.

Being open-minded also needs to be distinguished from being prepared to compromise, where mutual concessions are made to reach agreement. There are limits here: "We cannot enter into compromises with the persons who argue that coloured individuals ought to be exterminated."[23] Yet compromise positions are attractive, no doubt because it is often the case that the open-minded person is willing to make concessions. But this is not done in an arbitrary way. Consider, however, the recent suggestion that, concerning curriculum disputes, it may be a good idea "to try as much as possible to adjust balances in ways which pacify those who seem most offended at current arrangements."[24] This proposal is open to the obvious objection that it takes no account of whether or not the arrangements give reasonable cause for offence. It is notorious that people can take offence at what is harmless. Furthermore, any policy based on this idea would be open to abuse by anyone who chose to exaggerate how much he had been offended. The notion of "giving the offended group a piece of the action"[25] may have a liberal ring to it, but it is significant that this is immediately connected with the idea of finding compromise solutions. To take this view is surely to head in the direction of limp relativism.[26] If each and every view is to be reckoned in to avoid giving offence, we abandon the distinction between views which *deserve* serious attention and those which do not.

The point here is seen most clearly in connection with the now fashionable *equal time* theories. It must, of course, be admitted that this slogan has been useful in reminding us that there are rival views to be considered, and that these have often been neglected or even suppressed. Many, perhaps most, educators would concur with the view that "a system of public education sympathetic to a legitimate cultural diversity demands standards drawn from more than one culture."[27] But although the slogan has been valuable in this way, it cannot be accepted literally as a guide to curriculum planning. Equal time theories mean that any notion of the more and less important or significant in education must be abandoned, since all views are to receive the same attention. But this surely comes into conflict with a central aim of education, which is to foster a sense of what is important and significant. It is true that within an equal time framework, teachers could argue that certain views were really insignificant. But the hidden message conveyed by equal time would undermine this. Presumably, we are tempted in the direction of equal time theories by the principles of fairness and respect for the views of others. But then, these same principles will suggest some limit also, for example, in connection with views which call for, and show, disrespect for other groups. And is it fair to our students to waste their time on fatuous ideas?

We may consider finally a suggestion for effecting a compromise which involves a pluralism in which groups are permitted to design an education which reflects the values of the particular group. One argument for this is based on the importance of group maintenance and attempts to justify those parents who do not wish their children to be exposed to certain ideas: "If one believes in a pluralist society, he ought also to believe that groups have the right to perpetuate themselves over generations ... The right of groups to such self-perpetuation assumes that groups have the right to design an education which initiates the child into group norms and protects him from influences which lead astray."[28] It is certainly important to remind ourselves that the market-place of ideas may not in fact give certain groups a fair chance to present their point of view. Nevertheless, the case has been overstated. The groups in question have a right to try to attract adherents, not a right to adopt any means which will ensure their success. Groups must be free to present their views in a way which permits the young person to make a reasonable choice. Open-mindedness does not require that we sanction indoctrination.

CONCLUSION

This final chapter has drawn the dismal moral that the ideal of open-mindedness is not even safe from its professed friends. In recent years, the attitude has been invoked in support of a movement which has sought to have certain ideas excluded from the curriculum, and this has led to important theories and excellent books being condemned.[29] The paradox is that some have practised censorship in the name of open-mindedness. The enormous problems surrounding censorship have led other educational theorists to offer a wide variety of liberal-sounding suggestions. But all of these, attractive as they may appear as solutions to the censorship dilemma, fail to satisfy that fundamental commitment to rational appraisal which is the hallmark of open-mindedness.

Notes

CHAPTER ONE

1 This example was suggested to me by Olivier Reboul.
2 See Noam Chomsky, letter to the editor, *The Guardian* (England), 10 February 1981.
3 G.J. Warnock, "Education and Pluralism: What Sort of Problems?" *Oxford Review of Education* 1, no. 2 (1975): 95.
4 John Colbeck, "Criticising Critical Philosophy of Education," *Journal of Further and Higher Education* 4, no. 2 (Summer 1980): 64.
5 Ibid.
6 Ibid.
7 Gerhert Niemeyer, "Problems of Teaching about Communism," in Byron G. Massialas and Andreas M. Kazamias, eds., *Crucial Issues in the Teaching of Social Studies* (Englewood Cliffs, NJ: Prentice-Hall 1964), 194. A variant on Niemeyer's mistake is the error of thinking that a critical response to an argument implies that the argument responded to has some merit; cf. D.A. MacIver, "Can Linguistic Philosophers Teach Teachers Anything Worthwhile?" *Teacher Education* 5 (Spring 1972): 44–9.
8 E.g., Mary Warnock, "The Neutral Teacher," in S.C. Brown, ed., *Philosophers Discuss Education* (Totowa: Rowman and Littlefield 1975), 169; and D.Z. Phillips, "Not in Front of the Children: Children and the Heterogeneity of Morals," *Journal of the Philosophy of Education* 14, no. 1 (1980): 74.
9 Warnock, "The Neutral Teacher," 169.
10 Colbeck, "Criticising Critical Philosophy," 66.
11 See, for example, Stewart Candlish, "The Origins of Scepticism," *Journal of Moral Education* 4, no. 3 (June 1975): 199.
12 D.Z. Phillips and H.O. Mounce, *Moral Practices* (London: Routledge and Kegan Paul 1970), 105–6.

13 Joel Feinberg, "The Idea of a Free Man," in James Doyle, ed., *Educational Judgments* (London: Routledge and Kegan Paul 1973), 166.

14 Peter Unger, *Ignorance* (Oxford: Clarendon Press 1975), 115–16.

15 David Bridges, *Education, Democracy and Discussion* (Windsor: NFER Publishing Company 1979), 56.

16 Unger, *Ignorance*, 105.

17 Cf. Alan R. White, "On Claiming to Know," *Philosophical Review* 66 (1957): 180–92.

18 Charles Peirce, "The Fixation of Belief," *Popular Science Monthly*, November 1877.

19 Plato, *Meno* 84C.

20 Colbeck, "Criticising Critical Philosophy," 66.

21 J.E. Colbeck, "The Vulgar Component in Philosophy," *Education for Teaching* no. 99 (Spring 1976): 24.

22 Colbeck, "Criticising Critical Philosophy," 60.

23 Ibid., 66.

24 Ibid.

25 Cf. R.F. Holland, "Philosophers Discuss Education," *Philosophy* 52 (1977): 63–81. "Not much enthusiasm for this educational ideal was generated in me I confess by Dearden's list of the activities characteristic of the autonomous man" (64).

26 Colbeck, "Criticising Critical Philosophy," 67.

27 D.Z. Phillips, "Is Moral Education Really Necessary?" *British Journal of Educational Studies* 27, no. 1 (February 1979): 42–56.

28 Ibid., 52.

29 Warnock, "The Neutral Teacher," 168.

30 Plato, *Euthyphro*, 4A.

31 Colbeck, "Criticising Critical Philosophy," 64.

32 R.M. Hare, "Peace," in *Applications of Moral Philosophy* (London: Macmillan 1972), 80.

33 Colbeck, "Criticising Critical Philosophy," 60.

34 Plato, *Crito*.

35 Plato, *Apology* 35C.

36 Cf. G. Pitcher, "Emotion," in R.F. Dearden, P.H. Hirst, and R.S. Peters, eds., *Education and the Development of Reason* (London: Routledge and Kegan Paul 1972), 373.

37 Cf. Antony Flew, "The Jensen Uproar," *Philosophy* 48 (1973): 63–9.

38 See, for example, Kevin Harris, *Education and Knowledge* (London: Routledge and Kegan Paul 1979), 80.

39 Colbeck, "Criticising Critical Philosophy," 66.

40 This possibility is nicely satirized in Holland, "Philosophers," 65.

41 Phillips, "Moral Education," 50.

42 John Colbeck has returned to these themes in a recent paper, "The Need

for an Alternative Philosophy of Education," *Journal of Further and Higher Education* 8, no. 2 (1984): 39–52. But I do not think he has dealt with the major points advanced here.

43 John McPeck, *Critical Thinking and Education* (Don Mills: Oxford University Press 1981), 160.

CHAPTER TWO

1 See, for example, David Nyberg, ed., *The Philosophy of Open Education* (London: Routledge and Kegan Paul 1975), and Charles E. Silberman, ed., *The Open Classroom Reader* (New York: Vintage Books 1973).

2 These, and other concepts, are carefully examined in the context of elementary education in R.F. Dearden, *The Philosophy of Primary Education* (London: Routledge and Kegan Paul 1968).

3 One must not exaggerate. Certainly the idea is sometimes mentioned and said to be important. See, for example, Edward Victor and Marjorie S. Lerner, eds., *Readings in Science Education for the Elementary School*, 2nd ed. (New York: Macmillan 1971). But the concept is not carefully analysed and, as we shall see, misleading comments are made about it. See note 5 below.

4 These points are developed in my *Open-mindedness and Education* (Montreal: McGill-Queen's University Press 1979). I am grateful to Antony Flew for helpful comments on prejudice and bias.

5 It is sometimes claimed that open-mindedness is "closely akin to suspended judgment." See Richard E. Haney, "The Development of Scientific Attitudes," in Victor and Lerner, eds., *Readings*, 72.

6 H.J. McCloskey, "Liberalism," *Philosophy* 49 (1974): 13–32.

7 Ibid., 27.

8 Plato, *Meno*.

9 L. Kohlberg, "Stages of Moral Development as a Basis for Moral Education," in C.M. Beck et al., eds., *Moral Education: Interdisciplinary Approaches* (Toronto: University of Toronto Press 1971), 23–92. See in particular p. 36.

10 See Michael F.D. Young, ed., *Knowledge and Control* (London: Collier-Macmillan 1971).

11 Barry K. Beyer, *Inquiry in the Social Studies Classroom: A Strategy for Teaching* (Columbus: Charles E. Merrill 1971), 15–16.

12 See Robert Bierstedt, *Power and Progress* (New York: McGraw-Hill 1974), 154.

13 Descartes, *Meditations*, bk. 1.

14 Michael Oakeshott, "Learning and Teaching," in R.S. Peters, ed., *The Concept of Education* (London: Routledge and Kegan Paul 1967), 176.

15 Matthew Lipman, Ann Margaret Sharp, and Frederick S. Oscanyan, *Phi-*

losophy in the Classroom (Upper Montclair: The Institute for the Advancement of Philosophy for Children 1977).

16 See chap. 1, p. 4
17 McCloskey, "Liberalism," 27.

CHAPTER THREE

1 Hilary Putnam, "Comments on Chomsky's and Fodor's Replies," in Massimo Piattelli-Palmarini, ed., *Language and Learning: The Debate between Jean Piaget and Noam Chomsky* (Cambridge: Harvard University Press 1980), 336. Unfortunately, Putnam seems to adopt the view that open-mindedness implies neutrality or doubt. See further, note 30.
2 Cf. W.D. Hudson, "Trusting to Reason," *New Universities Quarterly* 33, no. 2 (1980): 251.
3 See my *Open-mindedness and Education* (Montreal: McGill-Queen's University Press 1979), chap. 3. A closed-minded person may, of course, be concerned to protect and preach what he *takes* to be the truth, but he lacks the concern in question which involves asking seriously if what he protects and promotes really is true.
4 Robin Barrow, *Moral Philosophy for Education* (London: George Allen and Unwin 1975), 207.
5 Plato, *Republic* 377.
6 See, for example, R.M. Hare, "Value Education in a Pluralist Society," *Proceedings of the Philosophy of Education Society of Great Britain* 10 (July 1976): 7-23.
7 R.M. Hare, "Ethical Theory and Utilitarianism," in H.D. Lewis, ed., *Contemporary British Philosophy* (London: Allen and Unwin 1976), 124.
8 Ibid., 123.
9 Ibid., 124. Hare now prefers to call the two levels the intuitive (level-1) and the critical (level-2). See R.M. Hare, *Moral Thinking: Its Levels, Method and Point* (Oxford: Clarendon Press 1981), 25.
10 G.E. Moore, *Principia Ethica* (London: Cambridge University Press 1903), 162-3.
11 R.M. Hare, "Ethical Theory," 124. Also R.M. Hare, "What is Wrong with Slavery?" *Philosophy and Public Affairs* 8, no. 2 (1979): 117.
12 See my "Controversial Issues and the Teacher," *High School Journal* 57, no. 2 (November 1973): 51-60.
13 R.M. Hare, "What is Wrong," 117.
14 R.M. Hare, "Ethical Theory," 124.
15 Moore, *Principia Ethica*, 151.
16 R.M. Hare, "Principles," *Proceedings of the Aristotelian Society* 72 (1972-3): 11.

17 R.M. Hare, "Rules of War and Moral Reasoning," *Philosophy and Public Affairs* 1, no. 2 (Winter 1972): 178.

18 R.M. Hare, "What is Wrong," 117.

19 R.M. Hare, *Freedom and Reason* (London: Oxford University Press 1963), 44.

20 See Godfrey Vesey, ed., *Philosophy in the Open* (Open University Press 1974), 51.

21 R.M. Hare, "On Terrorism," *The Journal of Value Inquiry* 13, no. 4 (1979): 246.

22 R.M. Hare, "Principles," 17.

23 R.M. Hare, "Rules of War," 178.

24 R.M. Hare, "Principles," 8. Cf. J.L. Mackie, *Ethics: Inventing Right and Wrong* (Harmondsworth: Penguin Books 1977), 139.

25 R.M. Hare, "What is Wrong," 117.

26 Ibid., 116.

27 Ibid., 117.

28 Mackie, *Ethics*, 156.

29 R.M. Hare, "Abortion and the Golden Rule," *Philosophy and Public Affairs* 4, no. 3 (Spring 1975): 216.

30 Cf. David Bridges, *Education, Democracy and Discussion* (Windsor: NFER Press 1979), 56, and Peter Unger, *Ignorance* (Oxford: Clarendon Press 1975), 115-16.

31 See Basil Mitchell, "Reason and Commitment in the Academic Vocation," *Oxford Review of Education* 2, no. 2 (1976): 101-9.

32 See Joel J. Kupperman, "Inhibition," *Oxford Review of Education* 4, no. 3 (1978): 277-87.

33 R.M. Hare, "Principles," 17.

34 Ibid.

35 Richard B. Brandt, *A Theory of the Good and the Right* (Oxford: Clarendon Press 1979), 275.

36 Cf. Joel J. Kupperman, "Vulgar Consequentialism," *Mind* 89 (July 1980): 332.

37 R.M. Hare, "Ethical Theory," 125.

38 Ibid.

39 Alan Montefiore, ed., *Neutrality and Impartiality: The University and Political Commitment* (London: Cambridge University Press 1975), 21.

40 Bridges, "Education," 70.

41 Brandt, *Theory of the Good*, 277. Cf. D.Z. Phillips and H.O. Mounce, *Moral Practices* (London: Routledge and Kegan Paul 1970), 84.

42 Ibid., 272.

43 Joel Feinberg, "The Idea of a Free Man," in James Doyle, ed., *Educational Judgments* (London: Routledge and Kegan Paul 1973), 166.

44 Moore, *Principia Ethica*, 162. Cf. Brandt, *Theory of the Good*, 274, and R.M. Hare, "Principles," 12.

45 R.M. Hare, "Value Education," 15.

46 Cf. Brandt, *Theory of the Good*, 78. He neglects to reintroduce this point, however, in the context of his criticism of act-utilitarianism.

47 Plato, *Crito* 47A.

48 Moore, *Principia Ethica*, 162. Cf. Mackie, *Ethics*, 156, and Brandt, *Theory of the Good*, 274.

49 Moore, *Principia Ethica*, 163.

50 Brandt, "Towards a Credible Utilitarianism," in Hector-Neri Castañeda and George Nakhnikian, eds., *Morality and the Language of Conduct* (Detroit: Wayne State University Press 1965), 116.

51 Plato, *Crito* 44C.

52 Brenda Cohen, "Principles and Situations: The Liberal Dilemma and Moral Education," in *Proceedings of the Aristotelian Society* 76 (1975–6): 79. Hare, indeed, clearly places *himself* in the group which ought to apply their level-1 principles rigidly. See "Ethical Theory," 129.

53 R.M. Hare, "Value Education," 12.

54 R.M. Hare, "Principles," 16. Cf. R.M. Hare, "Ethical Theory," 126.

55 R.M. Hare, "Can I Be Blamed for Obeying Orders?" in R.M. Hare, *Applications of Moral Philosophy* (London: Macmillan 1972), 8.

CHAPTER FOUR

1 See chap. 1.

2 See Harvey Siegel, "Rationality, Talking Dogs and Forms of Life," *Educational Theory* 30, no. 2 (1980): 136.

3 Allen T. Pearson, "The Competency Concept," *Educational Studies* 11, no. 2 (1980): 150–1.

4 Ibid., 151.

5 See my paper, "The Concept of Innovation in Education," *Educational Theory* 28, no. 1 (1978): 70.

6 W. James Popham, "Objectives and Instruction," in James A. Johnson et al., eds., *Foundations of American Education: Readings*, 2nd ed. (Boston: Allyn and Bacon 1972), 448–67. See in particular 455–6.

7 Popham, "Objectives and Instruction," 451.

8 See Edgar L. Morphet et al., *Educational Organization and Administration: Concepts, Practices and Issues*, 3rd ed. (Englewood Cliffs: Prentice-Hall 1974), 546.

9 On the assumption that the concept of education is value-laden, see R.S. Peters, *Ethics and Education* (London: George Allen and Unwin 1966), 25.

10 See Alexander Calandra, "Angels on a Pin," in Glenn Smith and Charles

R. Kniker, eds., *Myth and Reality: A Reader in Educational Foundations* (Boston: Allyn and Bacon 1972), 4–6.

11 R.F. Dearden, "The Assessment of Learning," *British Journal of Educational Studies* 27, no. 2 (June 1979): 114.

12 Ibid.

13 Neil Postman and Charles Weingartner, *Teaching as a Subversive Activity* (New York: Delta Books 1969), 35.

14 Michael F.D. Young, "School Science – Innovations or Alienation?" in Peter Woods and Martyn Hammersley, eds., *School Experience* (New York: St. Martin's Press 1977), 259.

15 Cf. Robin Barrow, *The Philosophy of Schooling* (Brighton: Wheatsheaf Books 1981), 193.

16 See Julia Evetts, *The Sociology of Educational Ideas* (London: Routledge and Kegan Paul 1973), 77.

17 Rodney A. Clifton and Ishmael J. Baksh, "Physical Attractiveness, Year of University, and the Expectations of Student-Teachers," *Canadian Journal of Education* 3, no. 3 (1978): 43.

18 Ibid., 42.

19 Robert Rosenthal and Lenore Jacobson, *Pygmalion in the Classroom* (New York: Holt, Rinehart and Winston 1968).

20 William Glasser, *Schools Without Failure* (New York: Harper and Row 1969).

21 James Herndon, *How to Survive in Your Native Land* (New York: Bantam Books 1972), 97.

22 For a balanced discussion of the reaction of the school to the creative student, see Liam Hudson, *Contrary Imaginations* (Harmondsworth: Pelican Books 1967), 133–5.

23 Sidney B. Simon, "Grades Must Go," *School Review* 78, no. 3 (1970): 397–402.

24 See R.S. Peters, "Education as Initiation," in R.D. Archambault, ed., *Philosophical Analysis and Education* (London: Routledge and Kegan Paul 1965), 87–111.

25 See Michael F.D. Young, "The Sociology of Knowledge: A Dialogue between John White and Michael Young," *Education for Teaching* 98 (1975): 7.

26 Ivan Illich, "The Alternative to Schooling," *Saturday Review*, 19 June 1971, 45.

27 Geoff Whitty, "Sociology and the Problem of Radical Educational Change," in Michael Flude and John Ahier, eds., *Educability, Schools and Ideology* (New York: John Wiley and Sons 1974), 119.

28 Young, "School Science," 261.

29 David Riesman et al., *Academic Values and Mass Education* (New York: McGraw-Hill 1970), 143.

30 See my *Open-mindedness and Education* (Montreal: McGill-Queen's University Press 1979).

31 Ralph Tyler, *Basic Principles of Curriculum and Instruction* (Chicago: University of Chicago Press 1949), 3.

32 Ronald T. Hyman, ed., *Approaches in Curriculum* (Englewood Cliffs: Prentice-Hall 1973), 8.

33 Morphet et al., *Educational Organization*, 546.

34 Alan R. White, *The Philosophy of Mind* (New York: Random House 1967): 154.

35 Popham, "Objectives and Instruction," 455.

36 Lawrence Stenhouse, *An Introduction to Curriculum Research and Development* (London: Heinemann 1975), 77.

37 Popham, "Objectives and Instruction," 455.

38 Ibid.

39 On the matter of there being a psychological limit to the complexity of principles in practice, see chap. 3, p. 31.

40 Stenhouse, *Introduction to Curriculum Research*, 79.

41 For a balanced discussion of creativity as an aim of teaching, see Don Cochrane, "Teaching and Creativity: A Philosophical Analysis," *Educational Theory* 25, no. 1 (1975): 65–73.

42 See my paper, "The Roles of Teacher and Critic," *Journal of General Education* 22, no. 1 (1970): 44. The point is argued in great detail in Antony Flew, "Teaching and Testing," reprinted in Antony Flew, *Sociology, Equality and Education* (London: The Macmillan Press 1976), 79–97.

43 John Holt, *What Do I Do Monday?* (New York: Dell Publishing Co. 1970), 236.

44 Dearden, "Assessment of Learning," 120.

45 See, for example, Harold Benjamin, *The Saber-Tooth Curriculum* (New York: McGraw-Hill 1939).

46 Young, "School Science," 261.

47 Whitty, "Sociology and Educational Change," 131.

48 Barrow, *Philosophy of Schooling*, 74.

49 Geoff Whitty, "Experiencing School Knowledge: The Case of the Social Studies," in Peter Woods and Martyn Hammersley, eds., *School Experience* (New York: St. Martin's Press 1977), 238.

50 Whitty, "Sociology and Educational Change," 122.

51 David Hume, *A Treatise of Human Nature*, bk. 1, pt. 3.

CHAPTER FIVE

1 See my *Open-mindedness and Education* (Montreal: McGill-Queen's University Press 1979).

2 Plato, *Meno*.

3 R.F. Dearden tends to neglect this point when he appeals to the "relative difference" argument in his "Autonomy and Education," in R.F. Dearden, P.H. Hirst, and R.S. Peters, eds., *Education and the Development of Reason* (London: Routledge and Kegan Paul 1972), 454.

4 Rachel Sharp, *Knowledge, Ideology and the Politics of Schooling: Towards a Marxist Analysis of Education* (London: Routledge and Kegan Paul 1980), 124.

5 The allusion, it hardly needs to be said, is to Ivan Illich. See "The Alternative to Schooling," *Saturday Review*, 19 June 1971.

6 Pierre Bourdieu and Jean-Claude Passeron, *Reproduction in Education, Society and Culture*, trans. Richard Nice (London: Sage Publications 1977), 109.

7 Ibid., 5.

8 Michael F.D. Young, "School Science – Innovations or Alienation?" in Peter Woods and Martin Hammersley, eds., *School Experience: Explorations in the Sociology of Education* (New York: St. Martin's Press 1977), 255.

9 Ibid., 260.

10 Alison M. Jaggar, "Male Instructors, Feminism and Women's Studies," *Teaching Philosophy* 2, nos. 3–4 (1977–8): 247–56.

11 Ibid., 250.

12 Edgar Z. Friedenberg, "Children as Objects of Fear and Loathing," *Educational Studies* 10, no. 1 (1979): 63–75.

13 Ibid., 71.

14 Edgar Z. Friedenberg, "Hegemony and the Process of Schooling: A Second Look at the Hidden Curriculum," *Teacher Education* 20 (April 1982); 29.

15 Bruce B. Suttle, "The Need for and Inevitability of Indoctrination," *Educational Studies* 12, no. 2 (1981): 154.

16 Ibid., 155.

17 W.I. McGucken, *The Catholic Way in Education* (Milwaukee: Bruce Publishing Company 1937), 60.

18 Lawrence Kohlberg, "Stages of Moral Development as a Basis for Moral Education," in C.M. Beck, B.S. Crittenden, and E.V. Sullivan, eds., *Moral Education: Interdisciplinary Approaches* (Toronto: University of Toronto Press 1971), 72.

19 Willis Moore, "Indoctrination and Democratic Method," in I.A. Snook, ed., *Concepts of Indoctrination* (London: Routledge and Kegan Paul 1972), 97. Also H.J. McCloskey, "Liberalism," *Philosophy* 49 (1974): 27.

20 For Socrates' views, see Plato, *Apology*. For Descartes' views, see *Discourse on Method*, chap. 1. It was apparently Descartes' unwillingness to be described as *teaching* the method which led him to use the word "dis-

course" rather than "traité" in the title. See letter to Mersenne, 27 February 1637, in A. Kenny, trans. and ed., *Descartes Philosophical Letters* (Oxford: Clarendon Press 1970), 30.

21 Israel Scheffler, *The Language of Education* (Springfield: Charles C. Thomas 1960), 57.

22 See chap. 2, p. 24.

23 John Holt, *Escape from Childhood* (New York: Ballantine Books 1974), 188. See also my critique in "Calling a Halt," *Educational Studies* 7, no. 1 (1976): 62–72.

24 See R.F. Dearden, "The Assessment of Learning," *British Journal of Educational Studies* 27, no. 2 (1979): 113.

25 Antonio Gramsci, "The Organization of Education and Culture" in *Prison Notebooks*, eds., Quintin Hoare and Geoffrey Nowell-Smith (New York: International Publishers 1971), 30.

26 Jaggar, "Male Instructors," 254.

27 Kurt Baier, *The Moral Point of View* (New York: Random House 1965), 160.

28 See R.F. Dearden, "Instruction and Learning by Discovery," in R.S. Peters, ed., *The Concept of Education* (London: Routledge and Kegan Paul 1967), 137.

CHAPTER SIX

1 Herbert A. Simon, *Administrative Behavior*, 2nd ed. (New York: The Free Press 1965), 20.

2 John McPeck, *Critical Thinking and Education* (Oxford: Martin Robertson 1981), 59.

3 See my *Open-mindedness and Education* (Montreal: McGill-Queen's University Press 1979), 11–12.

4 Simon, *Administrative Behavior*, 13.

5 Barnard's haunting example comes to mind of the telephone operator who remained at the switchboard though she could see her bedridden mother's house on fire. See Chester I. Barnard, *The Functions of the Executive* (Cambridge, Mass.: Harvard University Press 1938), 269.

6 Simon, *Administrative Behavior*, 36.

7 Plato, *Crito* 46B.

8 See also John Passmore, "On Teaching to Be Critical," in R.S. Peters, ed., *The Concept of Education* (London: Routledge and Kegan Paul 1967), 192–211.

9 See, for example, the views of Christopher Hodgkinson, *Towards a Philosophy of Administration* (Oxford: Basil Blackwell 1978), 5.

10 See also R.S. Peters, *Ethics and Education* (London: George Allen and Unwin 1966), 29.

11 Cf. Simon, *Administrative Behavior*, 45.

12 Ibid., 50.

13 See for example, Edgar L. Morphet et al., *Educational Organization and Administration*, 3rd ed. (Englewood Cliffs, NJ: Prentice-Hall 1974), 546.

14 See, for example, Michael F.D. Young, "The Sociology of Education," *Education for Teaching* 99 (1976): 51.

15 It is not even clear that the notions of truth and falsity do not apply to evaluative judgments in much the same way as they apply to factual ones. See Alan R. White, *Truth* (New York: Anchor Books 1970), 57–65.

16 Peters, *Ethics and Education*, 115.

17 R.M. Hare, *Freedom and Reason* (Oxford: Clarendon Press 1962), 109.

18 Descartes, *Discourse on Method*, pt. 2.

19 Robin Barrow, "Competence and the Head," in R.S. Peters, ed., *The Role of the Head* (London: Routledge and Kegan Paul 1976), 83.

20 Robert Dubin, "Union-Management Consultation," in Robert Dubin, ed., *Human Relations in Administration* (Englewood Cliffs, NJ: Prentice-Hall 1951), 312–18.

21 A.J. Bindman, "The Psychologist as a Mental Health Consultant," *Journal of Psychiatric Nursing* 2 (1964): 367–80. Cited in D. Brown et al., *Consultation: Strategy for Improving Education* (Boston: Allyn and Bacon 1979), 6.

22 George V. Mosher, "Consultative Management," in M.D. Richards and W.A. Nielander, eds., *Readings in Management*, 2nd ed. (New Rochelle, NY: South-Western Publishing Company 1963), 447–50.

23 Barrow, "Competence and the Head," 83–4.

24 Brown et al., *Consultation*, 7.

25 See Donna Kerr, *Educational Policy: Analysis, Structure, and Justification* (New York: David McKay 1976): 195.

26 Barnard, *Functions of the Executive*, 189.

27 Ibid., 193.

28 McPeck, *Critical Thinking and Education*, 60.

29 William K. Frankena, "Freedom: Responsibility and Decision," *Proceedings of the XIVth International Congress of Philosophy* (Vienna: Herder 1968), 145.

30 Simon, *Administrative Behavior*, 66.

31 Kerr, *Educational Policy*, 199.

32 Barnard, *Functions of the Executive*, 264.

33 William Hare, *Open-Mindedness and Education*, 60.

34 Cf. Robin H. Farquhar, "Preparing Educational Administrators for Ethical Practice," *Alberta Journal of Educational Research* 27, no. 2 (1981): 195.

35 Andrew W. Halpin, "Administrative Theory: The Fumbled Torch," in Arthur M. Kroll, ed., *Issues in American Education* (New York: Oxford University Press 1970), 178.

CHAPTER SEVEN

1 For examples of this general view, see Karl Popper, *Unended Quest* (Glasgow: Fontana/Collins 1976), 38; Bertrand Russell, *Mysticism and Logic* (Harmondsworth: Penguin Books 1953), 46; Israel Scheffler, *Science and Subjectivity* (New York: Bobbs-Merrill 1967), 2.

2 See, for example, Bertrand Russell, *Religion and Science* (New York: Oxford University Press 1961), 14; Michael Martin, *Concepts of Science Education* (Glenview, Ill.: Scott, Foresman and Company 1972), 7; Jerome A. Popp, "Teaching Science Scientifically," *Journal of Education* (Nova Scotia) 7, no. 2 (1981): 14.

3 On this point, see Bernard Barber, "Resistance by Scientists to Scientific Discovery," *Science* 134 (1961): 596–602, and Nicholas Rescher, "The Ethical Dimension of Scientific Research," in Eleanor Kuykendall, ed., *Philosophy in the Age of Crisis* (New York: Harper and Row 1970), 68–81.

4 Martin Gardner goes so far as to say that the myth of science as wholly rational is itself a myth. See his review in *Discover* 4, no. 4 (April 1983): 93. Gardner himself has done much to destroy the stereotypical view in his *Fads and Fallacies in the Name of Science* (New York: Dover Publications 1957).

5 The central work is Thomas S. Kuhn, *The Structure of Scientific Revolutions*, 2nd ed., enlarged (Chicago: University of Chicago Press 1970). All references are to this edition.

6 See, in particular, John W.N. Watkins, "Against 'Normal Science'," in I. Lakatos and A. Musgrave, eds., *Criticism and the Growth of Knowledge* (Cambridge: Cambridge University Press 1970), 27. Also Harvey Siegel, "Kuhn and Critical Thought," in Ira S. Steinberg, ed., *Philosophy of Education 1977: Proceedings* (Urbana: University of Illinois 1977), 173–9.

7 Jon Fennell and Rudy Liveritte, "Kuhn, Education, and the Grounds of Rationality," *Educational Theory* 29, no. 2 (1979): 122.

8 Of course, if indoctrination is inevitable, the question of prescribing it will not arise.

9 This strange objection is raised against Siegel by Fennell and Liveritte, apparently arising from a failure to appreciate the value of dealing with *possible* interpretations. See Fennell and Liveritte, "Kuhn, Education," 117n2.

10 Kuhn, *Structure of Scientific Revolutions*, chap. 4.

11 Watkins, "Against 'Normal Science'," 27.

12 Kuhn, in Lakatos and Musgrave, eds., *Criticism and the Growth of Knowledge*, 6.

13 Kuhn, *Structure of Scientific Revolutions*, 19.

14 Ibid., 24.

15 Ibid., 29. In taking these examples of open-mindedness from Kuhn's own

work, I am not trying to suggest that he presents them as such himself.

16 Ibid., 26.

17 These points tend to be ignored by Harvey Siegel in his "Kuhn and Critical Thought," 176–7.

18 See Fennell and Liveritte, "Kuhn, Education," 121, 125.

19 Fennell and Liveritte come close to this. See ibid., 120.

20 Joseph Priestley on phlogiston, and Lord Kelvin on the indivisibility of the atom, are favourite examples here.

21 Kuhn, *Structure of Scientific Revolutions*, 85, and elsewhere.

22 Ibid., 118.

23 Ibid., 148.

24 Ibid., 151.

25 Ibid., 9.

26 Hans Reichenbach, *Experience and Prediction* (Chicago: University of Chicago Press 1938).

27 Scheffler, *Science and Subjectivity*, 80.

28 Renford Bambrough, "Conflict and the Scope of Reason," *Ratio* 20, no. 2 (December 1978): 77–91.

29 See Hugo Meynell, "Science, the Truth, and Thomas Kuhn," *Mind* 84 (1975): 79–93.

30 N.R. Hanson, *Patterns of Discovery* (London: Cambridge University Press 1961).

31 Kevin Harris, *Education and Knowledge* (London: Routledge and Kegan Paul 1979), 10.

32 See Jonas F. Soltis, *Education and the Concept of Knowledge* (New York: Teachers College 1979), 7.

33 Harris, *Education and Knowledge*, 16.

34 Ibid., 17.

35 Scheffler, *Science and Subjectivity*, 84.

36 See Henry Frankel, review of Thomas S. Kuhn, *The Essential Tension*, in *Philosophy of Science* 45, no. 4 (1978): 651. The distinction compares with the ambiguity in the notion of "acceptance" pointed out by Scheffler in *Science and Subjectivity*, 86.

37 See Kuhn, *Structure of Scientific Revolutions*, 77.

38 Barber, "Resistance by Scientists," 596.

39 There are well-known historical and contemporary cases, and the names involved include the famous and respected.

40 There have been many statements of the self-referential problems in relativism. A particularly trenchant critique can be found in Harvey Siegel, "Relativism Refuted," *Educational Philosophy and Theory* 14, no. 2 (1982): 47–50.

41 J.S. Bruner and Leo Postman, "On the Perception of Incongruity: A Paradigm," *Journal of Personality* 18 (1949): 206–23.

42 Barber, "Resistance by Scientists," 598.

43 Barber himself is anxious to avoid the pessimistic conclusion. See ibid., 601.

44 The classic account is Martin Gardner, *Fads and Fallacies in the Name of Science*.

45 A notorious case is the judgment on J.J. Waterston's work by the Royal Society in the nineteenth century.

46 Kuhn, *Structure of Scientific Revolutions*, 65.

47 See my *Open-mindedness and Education* (Montreal: McGill-Queen's University Press 1979), chap. 2.

48 Thomas S. Kuhn, "The Function of Dogma in Scientific Research," A.C. Crombie, ed., *Scientific Change* (London: Heinemann 1963), 347–69.

49 Ibid., 348.

50 Stephen Toulmin, "Does the Distinction between Normal and Revolutionary Science Hold Water?" in Lakatos and Musgrave, eds., *Criticism and the Growth of Knowledge*, 40.

51 Kuhn, *Structure of Scientific Revolutions*, 25. Some of Kuhn's critics, who accept this point about the value of tenacity, are too ready to accept the appropriateness of the description in terms of dogmatism. See, for example, Watkins, "Against 'Normal Science'," 28.

52 Harvey Siegel, "Kuhn and Schwab on Science Texts and the Goals of Science Education," *Educational Theory* 28, no. 4 (1978): 307.

53 John Dewey, *Democracy and Education* (1916; reprint, New York: The Free Press 1966), 175.

54 Siegel, "Kuhn and Schwab," 307.

55 Kuhn, "Function of Dogma," 359.

56 Dewey, *Democracy and Education*, 176.

57 Kuhn, "Function of Dogma," 364.

58 Michael Polanyi, *Science, Faith and Society* (Chicago: University of Chicago Press 1964), 94.

59 Michael Polanyi, Commentary on Kuhn's "The Function of Dogma in Scientific Research," in Crombie, ed., *Scientific Change*, 380.

60 Polanyi, *Science, Faith and Society*, 57.

61 Ibid., 68. For important differences between open-mindedness and tolerance, see my "Open-mindedness in the Teaching of Philosophy," *Metaphilosophy* 13, no. 2 (1982): 165–80.

62 Thomas S. Kuhn, Response to Commentaries on Kuhn's "The Function of Dogma on Scientific Research," in Crombie, ed., *Scientific Change*, 393.

63 R.G. Woods and R. St.C. Barrow, *An Introduction to Philosophy of Education* (London: Methuen 1975), 73.

64 Kuhn, Response to Commentaries, 390.

65 Joseph J. Schwab, *The Teaching of Science as Enquiry* (Cambridge: Harvard University Press 1962).

66 Kuhn, Response to Commentaries, 391.
67 Schwab, *Teaching of Science*, 24.
68 See B. Glass, Discussion of Kuhn's "The Function of Dogma in Scientific Research," in Crombie, ed., *Scientific Change*, 381.
69 See Harvey Siegel, "On the Distortion of the History of Science in Science Education," *Science Education* 63, no. 1 (1979): 111–18.
70 The point derives from John Stuart Mill, *On Liberty*, chap. 2. It has more recently been made by Paul Feyerabend in "Democracy, Elitism and Scientific Method," *Inquiry* 23, no. 1 (1980): 3–18.
71 See an excerpt from *Education and the Spirit of Science* (1966), in Edward Victor and Marjorie S. Lerner, eds., *Readings in Science Education for the Elementary School* (New York: Macmillan 1971), 6–14.

CHAPTER EIGHT

1 Descartes, *Letter from the Author* (to the translator of the *Principles of Philosophy*).
2 John Stuart Mill, *On Liberty*, chap. 2.
3 David Bridges, *Education, Democracy and Discussion* (Windsor: NFER Publishing Company 1979), 49. But contrast p. 37.
4 Kenneth Strike, "Liberality and Censorship: A Philosophy of Textbooks Controversies," in Ira S. Steinberg, ed., *Philosophy of Education* (1977), 280.
5 Ibid., 278.
6 Ibid., 280.
7 Ibid.
8 Ibid.
9 Ibid., 280–1.
10 See, for example, R.A. Smith and J. Knight, "MACOS in Queensland: The Politics of Educational Knowledge," *Australian Journal of Education* 22, no. 3 (October 1978): 225–48.
11 Mill, *On Liberty*, chap. 2.
12 Barry Bull, "The Constitution, Liberal Theory, and Textbook Bias," *Educational Forum* 44, no. 2 (January 1980): 158.
13 Cf. Gary D. Glenn, "Partisanship and Neutrality in Teaching American Government," *Teaching Political Science* 6, no. 3 (April 1979): 311–30.
14 Bull, "The Constitution and Textbook Bias," 158.
15 Ibid., 155.
16 Lawrence Stenhouse, "An Appeal for Evidence of the Effectiveness of an Alternative Role to That of Neutral Chairman in Promoting Rational Inquiry into Moral Issues: A Reply to John T. Hyland," *Journal of Further and Higher Education* 1, no. 2 (Summer 1977): 53.
17 John Wilson, "Education and the Neutrality of the Teacher," *Journal of*

Christian Education 14, no. 3 (December 1971): 178.

18 Cf. John Kleinig, "Neutrality in Moral Education: A Rejoinder," *Journal of Christian Education* 14, no. 3 (December 1971): 150.

19 D.Z. Phillips, "A Freedom to Communicate: Censorship and the Life of the Intellect," *New Universities Quarterly* 32, no. 4 (Autumn 1978): 395.

20 Plato, *Meno* 89C.

21 Douglas Stewart, review of *Open-mindedness and Education* in *C.S.S.E. News*, December 1980, 15.

22 R.M. Hare, "Language and Moral Education," in Glenn Langford and D.J. O'Connor, eds., *New Essays in the Philosophy of Education* (London: Routledge and Kegan Paul 1973), 156.

23 H.J. McCloskey, "Liberalism," *Philosophy* 49 (1974): 13–32.

24 Strike, "Liberalism and Censorship," 285.

25 Ibid., 280.

26 Phillips, "Freedom to Communicate," 388.

27 Richard Pratte, "Cultural Diversity and Education," in Kenneth A. Strike and Kieran Egan, eds., *Ethics and Educational Policy* (London: Routledge and Kegan Paul 1978), 162.

28 Strike, "Liberality and Censorship," 283.

29 For further illustration of this, in connection with literature, see my paper, "Bias in Stories for Children: Black Marks for Authors," *Journal of Applied Philosophy* 2, no. 1 (1985): 99–108.

Bibliography

Bambrough, Renford. "Conflict and the Scope of Reason." *Ratio* 20, no. 2 (1978): 77–91.

Barber, Bernard. "Resistance by Scientists to Scientific Discovery." *Science* 134 (1961): 596–602.

Beveridge, W.I.B. *Seeds of Discovery*. New York: Norton 1980.

Beyerstein, Dale. "Skepticism, Closed-mindedness and Science fiction." *The Skeptical Inquirer* 6, no. 4 (1982): 47–53.

Blackham, H.J. *Humanism*. Harmondsworth: Penguin Books 1968.

Broad, William, and Wade, Nicholas. *Betrayers of the Truth*. New York: Simon and Schuster 1982.

Carter, Robert. *Dimensions of Moral Education*. Toronto: University of Toronto Press 1984.

Cochrane, Donald B., and Schiralli, Martin, eds. *Philosophy of Education: Canadian Perspectives*. Don Mills: Collier-Macmillan 1982.

Colbeck, John. "Criticising Critical Philosophy of Education." *Journal of Further and Higher Education* 4, no. 2 (1980): 60–72.

– "The Need for an Alternative Philosophy of Education." *Journal of Further and Higher Education* 8, no. 2 (1984): 39–52.

Corbett, J.P. "Opening the Mind." In *The Idea of a New University*, edited by David Daiches, 22–9. London: André Deutsch 1964.

Gardner, Martin. *Science: Good, Bad and Bogus*. Buffalo: Prometheus Books 1982.

Gould, Stephen Jay. *The Mismeasure of Man*. New York: Norton 1981.

Green, Thomas F. "A Topology of the Teaching Concept." In *Studies in Philosophy and Education* 3, no. 4 (1964–5): 285–319.

Hare, R.M. *Moral Thinking: Its Levels, Method and Point*. Oxford: Clarendon Press 1981.

Hare, William. *Open-mindedness and Education*. Montreal: McGill-Queen's University Press 1979.

- "The Attack on Open-mindedness." *Oxford Review of Education* 7, no. 2 (1981): 119–29.
- "Open-mindedness in the Teaching of Philosophy." *Metaphilosophy* 13, no. 2, (1982): 165–80.
- "Standards as a Threat to Open-mindedness." *European Journal of Teacher Education* 5, no. 3 (1982): 133–45.
- "Open-mindedness in Elementary Education." *Elementary School Journal* 83, no. 3 (1983): 212–19.
- "Open-mindedness, Liberalism and Truth." *Educational Philosophy and Theory* 15, no. 1 (1983): 31–42.
- *Controversies in Teaching.* London, Ont.: The Althouse Press 1985.
- , ed. *Journal of Education* (Nova Scotia), 7, no. 2 (1981). Special issue on the philosophy of education.
Hudson, W.D. "Trusting to reason." *New Universities Quarterly* 31, no. 2 (1980): 241–57.
Hull, John M. "Open Minds and Empty Hearts." In *Approaching World Religions*, edited by Robert Jackson, 101–10. London: Murray 1982.
Klapp, Orrin E. *Opening and Closing: Strategies of Information Adaptation in Society.* Cambridge: Cambridge University Press 1978.
Kuhn, Thomas S. *The Structure of Scientific Revolutions.* Chicago: University of Chicago Press 1962.
- "The Function of Dogma in Scientific Research." In *Scientific Change*, edited by A.C. Crombie, 347–69. London: Heinemann 1963.
Kurtz, Paul. "Debunking, Neutrality and Skepticism." *The Skeptical Inquirer* 8, no. 3 (1984): 239–46.
Lloyd, Ieuan. "Teaching Religious Understanding." *Religious Studies* 17, no. 2 (1981): 253–9.
McPeck, John E. *Critical Thinking and Education.* Oxford: Martin Robertson 1981.
Martin, Everett Dean. *The Meaning of a Liberal Education.* New York: Norton 1926.
Mitchell, Basil. "Religious Education." *Oxford Review of Education* 6, no. 2 (1980): 133–9.
Mittens, W.H. "Teaching and the Illusion of Certainty." *Durham and Newcastle Research Review* 9, no. 48 (Spring 1982): 344–53.
Moore, Richard W. "Open-mindedness and Proof." *School Science and Mathematics* 82, no. 6 (1982): 478–80.
Newman, Jay. *Foundations of Religious Tolerance.* Toronto: University of Toronto Press 1982.
Phillips, D.Z. "A Freedom to Communicate: Censorship and the Life of the Intellect." *New Universities Quarterly* 32, no. 4 (Autumn 1978): 387–401.
Reber, Arthur S. "On the Paranormal: In Defense of Skepticism." *The Skeptical Inquirer* 7, no. 2 (1982–3): 55–64.

Reboul, Olivier. *L'Endoctrinement*. Vendôme: Presses Universitaires de France 1977.

Siegel, Harvey. "Critical Thinking as an Educational Ideal." *Educational Forum* 45, no. 1 (1980): 7–23.

Simpson, Douglas J., and Jackson, Michael J.B. *The Teacher as Philosopher*. Toronto: Methuen 1984.

Soltis, Jonas. *Education and the Concept of Knowledge*. New York: Teachers College 1979.

– "On the Nature of Educational Research," *Educational Researcher* 13, no. 10 (1984): 5–10.

Strike, Kenneth. *Liberty and Learning*. Oxford: Martin Robertson 1982.

Wilder, Hugh T. "Tolerance and Teaching Philosophy." *Metaphilosophy* 9, nos. 3–4 (1978): 311–23.

Wilson, Bryan R. *Rationality*. New York: Harper 1970.

Index